Xpo

WHAT BELIEVERS OUGHT TO BELIEVE

William A. Mundhausen

Orion Center
Camdenton, Missouri

Copyright © 2014 by William A. Mundhausen.

All rights reserved. No part of this publication may be reproduced, distributed or transmitted in any form or by any means, including photocopying, recording, or other electronic or mechanical methods, without the prior written permission of the publisher, except in the case of brief quotations embodied in critical reviews and certain other noncommercial uses permitted by copyright law. For permission requests, write to the publisher, addressed "Attention: Permissions Coordinator," at the address below.

William A. Mundhausen/Orion Center
1163 S. Business Hwy 5, P.O. Box 1733
Camdenton, MO 65020
www.orioncenter.org

Book Layout ©2013 BookDesignTemplates.com

Ordering Information:
Quantity sales. Special discounts are available on quantity purchases by corporations, associations, and others. For details, contact the author at the address above.

Xpo: What Believers Ought To Believe/ William A. Mundhausen. —1st ed.
ISBN 978-0-6922629-0-0

Contents

Introduction 1
What's Your Worldview? 3
   One Of Us Is Crazy 3
   What Is A Worldview? 7
   What Effects Come From Worldviews? 11
   How Does Worldview Come About? 17
   Can A Worldview Change? 19
   Is A Biblical Worldview Viable? 22
What The Bible Says 27
   The Problem of Biblical Interpretation 27
   Objections To Reading The Bible Plainly 29
   Why Read The Bible Plainly? 31
   The Bible Story 33
   Future Prophesy And World Events 37
The Nature Of The Universe 41
   The Allure Of The Cosmos 41
   What Scientists Observe 44

    The Standard Cosmology 46

    What Scripture Says 48

    Creationist Cosmology 51

    Other Signs Of Design 55

The Story of Life 71

    We Call Them Creatures 71

    What Scientists Observe About Life 72

    The Evolutionary Tale 76

    What Scripture Says 77

    The Biblical View Of Life 80

    The Fascinating Creatures Chronicles 83

Geology And The Flood 95

    First Salvo In The Scientific War With God 95

    What Scientists Observe 102

    Evolutionary Geology 104

    What Scripture Tells Us 106

    Creationist Geology - The Hydroplate Theory 110

    Earth's Anomalies 113

Dragons And Dinosaurs 117

    What Do We Know About Dinosaurs? 117

    What Do We Know About Dragons? 120

    Which Is Which 124

The American Experiment In Biblical Government 127

    Give Us A King 127

    The Founders Brought Forward: It's Worldview Again 129

    Biblical Government Equitable For All 131

    Irreconcilable 140

The Christian Gospel 145

    What Is The Gospel? 145

    How Should We Then Live? 148

Conclusion 155

Bibliography 159

Index 161

To my wife, Peggy, who encouraged me to write this book

I call heaven and earth to witness against you today, that I have set before you life and death, the blessing and the curse. So choose life in order that you may live, you and your descendants, by loving the Lord your God, by obeying His voice, and by holding fast to Him; for this is your life and the length of your days.
—Deuteronomy 30:19-20

Introduction

Lord, make me an instrument of thy peace; where there is hatred, let me sow love; where there is injury, pardon; where there is doubt, faith; where there is darkness, light; and where there is sadness, joy. O Divine Master, grant that I may not so much seek to be consoled as to console; to be understood, as to understand; to be loved, as to love; for it is in giving that we receive, it is in pardoning that we are pardoned, and it is in dying that we are born to eternal life. - Francis of Assisi, Italy, 13th century

I Began writing this book on the eve of Thanksgiving as millions of Americans prepare to give thanks to the God who provides our many blessings. It is in fact a season of blessing as we prepare to celebrate the birth of Christ and the hope of a new year. Nevertheless, there are many others who are confused or even in rebellion against faith, the kind of nation we will be, and even such basic realities as the definition of family. We are a deeply divided people. Unfortunately, few are speaking with any clarity on any of our deepest values. The issue is TRUTH; what is true, and what do we do about it.

Thirteen years ago, I began to create what has become a Biblical worldview center. CreationXpo has a mission unlike other institutions; to explore America's roots in the founding of government, to renew belief in a Creator God, and to restore the dream of individual liberty; and to subsequently rediscover TRUTH. Simply put, CreationXpo is a ministry to America restoring the hearts of the people to God so that we can enjoy the continuing blessings that our nation's founders attributed to Him.

As I read that opening paragraph, it seems kind of lofty and abstract, but my purpose in writing this book, and the inspiration for CreationXpo, is very personal and practical. I read a blog today about the millennials, today's young adults, and their exodus from the church. The youthful author wrote, " When I returned to church, it wasn't because of great programs, alluring events or a really cool 'café' set up in the foyer. I went back not because of what the church was doing, but rather in spite of it. I went back because I needed community." That yearning to belong, to be a part of something bigger than myself, is something I can relate to. A couple of years ago I wrote down my lifetime goals, one of which was, "to work in a collaborative team environment to discuss, research. and implement eternal goals." Isn't that what church should be about, a collaboration of believers united in a common purpose to serve Jesus Christ." That's community, and that's something way bigger than myself.

My name is Bill Mundhausen. I'm a second-generation American born of German parents who immigrated to the United States during the Great Depression. I have always felt like someone who admired America more as an outsider than as a citizen. Perhaps it's just my analytical nature. When I accepted Jesus Christ as my Lord, I set sail on a journey of discovery not unlike every other believer I've known. My partner in this is my wife, Peggy, the love of my life as well as my guide and confidant along the way. We both have retained a love for those who never set sail, and we pray that just a few skeptics at least read about our God expedition even if they never choose to come along.

Not everyone decides to build a museum, but fourteen years ago I was inspired to take some of the wealth God blessed me with and create something for His glory, the Orion Science Center. It hasn't turned out like I envisioned but rather turned into what He envisioned. We like to say that God never changes, yet God is all about change when it comes to us and our finite attempts at achievement. Orion Center has been a series of scientific tests to refine the weapons of what is really spiritual warfare. Ultimately, Orion Center was transformed into a Biblical worldview center we call Creation Xpo. The Xpo is not a big impressive museum, but it has nevertheless been the inspiration for this book and the title, Xpo, What Believers Ought To Believe. Through these pages, I hope to convey something of the quest for God's truth, a quest that is as relevant for skeptics as it is for lovers of God.

CHAPTER 1

What's Your Worldview?

One Of Us Is Crazy

The Spirit of the sovereign Lord is on me, because the Lord has anointed me to proclaim good news to the poor. He has sent me to bind up the brokenhearted, to proclaim freedom for the captives, and release from darkness for the prisoners. - Isaiah 61:1 fulfilled by Jesus about 30 AD

One of us is crazy. There are essentially two "camps" of people in the world into which all the vast variety of people can be placed. One camp believes in a transcendent God overseeing the affairs of the world. The other does not, either worshipping pagan gods or substitutes. One believes that God created all things. The other believes no Creator was necessary; all things developed autonomously by natural processes. One believes in life after death. The other believes that now is all there is.

The concept we're talking about is "worldview", although I really wish I could coin a new name for it. The "worldview" label makes the issue seem philosophical when in fact it is very practical..."earthy" in fact. There are people who worship the earth and all that is in it, and those who worship the Creator of all things. So close, and yet so far! I'm talking about a conflict that is unintended but fundamental. The people in these "camps" don't necessarily consider themselves to be in two opposing movements. They don't even recognize that they are in a group most of the time. Yet all the world's people fit in one of these two groups and consider folks in the other group as "crazy".

The root of the matter is revealed in how we look at ordinary things or, for that matter, whether we believe anything is truly ordinary. Let's talk baseball, because nothing can be more ordinary and down-to-earth than America's pastime. There is an old video clip saved from the 1950's showing the great Willie Mays running deep into the cavernous centerfield at the Polo Grounds with his back to home plate catching the ball after it passes over his head and then whirling and slinging the ball back toward the infield. When did Willie start running? Was it after he saw the hit and gave his brain a moment to calculate its trajectory that set his body in motion? Or was it earlier when the crack of the bat and motion of the swing clued him in to anticipating the ball's flight? Or is there an as yet unknown sixth sense that accounts for a miraculous prescience that lets the fielder perform what seems impossible? Anyone who has played sports has experienced the feeling of doing something extraordinary. We don't do it as often as professional athletes, but it happens and we're amazed by it. It's like a flash of lightning, a tiny miracle, or an unexpected gift.

There is an amazing beauty in humanity, just as there is in the world around us, and it's a poor human being who isn't often touched by it. We see it in a young mother spending an extra moment to comfort a crying child. We revel in a feeling of exhilaration when justice triumphs over injustice. We experience a reverent hush when families mourn at the funeral of someone they loved. Life is something to cherish. We don't worship humanity however, but rather the Creator of humanity who crafted mankind in His image. We human beings are mere reflections of the true source of beauty, and believers are awed by that revelation.

Nevertheless, there are some people, members of that other "camp" who believe that all of experience is just the random working of time, matter and, energy. For purposes of this book, I'll ignore the pagan religions and focus on Western culture and the philosophy of humanism. Let's agree about how we should name these people. Some in my circle of Christian creationists would call them "evolutionists", but that's probably too narrow. They could be called any of the following: materialists, atheists, secularists, progressives, skeptics, agnostics, or anti-religionists. For my purposes, I will call them "humanists" because that term describes their core philosophy. A humanist believes that mankind is the ultimate authority, there is no higher intelligence, and that God is inadequate to be an explanation for the world around him. That means the universe created and maintains itself, and that only immense time and material churning is responsible for the end result. Man therefore is merely part of nature, a trivial byproduct of the cosmos. The term "humanist" is therefore ironic in that a humanist puts man at the top while simultaneously assigning man the position of being a mere cog in the vast machine of the cosmos. Mankind is not a reflection of someone greater than himself. He is merely "stardust" as Carl Sagan once put it.

For such as these, the beauty we see, the graceful precision of an athlete, the nuances of tone and melody produced by a great musical composer, the exquisite design of the natural environment...all are just artifacts of mindless process strained through the focus of vast amounts of time. This isn't just an abstract philosophical matter. It affects our most intimate and cherished needs. For example, everyone has a need to be loved and love in return. What does the love of a man and a woman mean to a humanist? Love is a biochemical reaction to pheromones and other stimuli that persists for a limited amount of time. The object of romantic love has been placed in our path by chance, and the only goal of this relationship is the instinctive perpetuation of our genetic material. The process of romantic love (and doesn't it sound romantic so far?) temporarily suspends our ability to reason because of the powerful chemical stimuli in our bodies and brains, but we know that the effect is transient and the meaning is not at all profound. After all, we are just biological machines. There is no soul or spirit, only flesh and hormones. Rationally, love, in a higher transcendent sense, is an illusion. We may trick ourselves into thinking we love the other person, but it is just our selfish needs playing themselves out for a while. How does one live in such a world?

Most humanists can't cope with the rational conclusions of their worldview, so they avoid thinking about such things. If they thought about the significance of their perspective about life, they would find themselves without ultimate hope. They would be forced to turn to humanist solutions to merely meet their needs. Their "god" becomes collective humanity; reliance on government for solutions to moral problems and dependence on friends and good times to make everyday life seem meaningful. It's not necessarily a bad life. It's simply what it is.

In the other camp, my camp, are believers in God. Believers have a different idea about Willie Mays. We believe he was made in God's image and that a tiny spark of God is what enables Willie and all of us to do extraordinary things. We don't see the world's beauty as an illusion, but rather as a true representation of a creation designed to be beautiful and glorifying as opposed to merely functional. What is love? Love is a spiritual experience in which we see the soul and spirit of another person as God sees them. We are therefore drawn to cherish the other person in a way that we don't fully understand but we recognize to be real and permanent. Yes, all the earthly biochemical factors are real, but they are icing on the cake of the more profound reality underlying them. In other words, we were created as physical beings, but each of us contains a spiritual seed revealing to us that our mere mechanical parts are inadequate to explain the whole.

So there it is. The two camps of mankind, humanists and theists, locked in permanent conflict, each with a different frame of reference and therefore rejecting the other's "god". They are at war because each camp's most foundational system of thought is diametrically opposed to the other camp. There is no basis for compromise.

Examine any conflict and you will find members of these two camps on opposite sides. In politics, humanists tend to be liberal left while theists conservative right. There is more irony in that humanists, in elevating Man, actually diminish the individual liberty of Man because the highest power in humanism is the collective rather than the individual. The individual is a serf subject to masters who are merely serfs to other men. Theism, on the other hand, sees the individual made in God's image as sacred and therefore autonomous within God's framework. Sorry to get all philosophical on you, but I'm trying to make it clear that this is not just a philosophical issue. The matter of whether you depend on the providence of God or the authority of human government affects your rights and freedoms in a very personal way. Is there hope for mediating between humanists and theists? No, they are opposing worldviews with committed adherents in each camp. But there is hope for those who haven't yet chosen a side or are open to searching for the truth. Through the remainder of this chapter we will flesh out what a worldview is, what fruits worldviews produce, how worldviews develop, and how they are changed.

What Is A Worldview?

During his first term in office, President Obama delivered a series of speeches in which he quoted the Declaration of Independence. Wishing to invoke a patriotic theme, he referred to America as a nation in which "we are all created equal and endowed with certain rights…" What he left out of course is that we are endowed "by our Creator" with those inalienable rights. Why did he leave out "by our Creator" in multiple speeches over several weeks? As a reputed constitutional scholar, it seems unlikely that the omission of "God" was accidental. Undoubtedly he strategically omitted reference to a creator because much of his constituency would be offended by the idea of a Creator God.

The idea that our rights come from God is profoundly important. When America's founders crafted the Declaration, they were in the process of defying the most powerful government on earth and offered the only justification for their rebellion. Governments do not give rights…they only either protect or violate them. "By our Creator" is a phrase that defines three areas of human experience. It is a scientific statement that frames our fundamental ideas about the nature of reality and the physical world as created and not simply material. It is a religious statement that proclaims our faith in a supreme being. America was founded as a Christian nation. Those two factors combine to determine the third area of experience, our views about society and government. We believe in limiting government and the power of men because men are fallen sinners. We also uphold individual liberty because men are made in God's image and are worthy of respect.

We use a simple triangle graphic to illustrate what we believe are the three primary aspects of a worldview. One aspect is what you believe about the material world. Another aspect of worldview is what you believe spiritually. Finally, there is the aspect of how you relate to people, society, and government. I have struggled to decide which of the three aspects should be the foundational one since the triangle draws us in to put one aspect at the base. As a Christian, I want to put faith and spirituality as the base, because I want to honor God. However, I

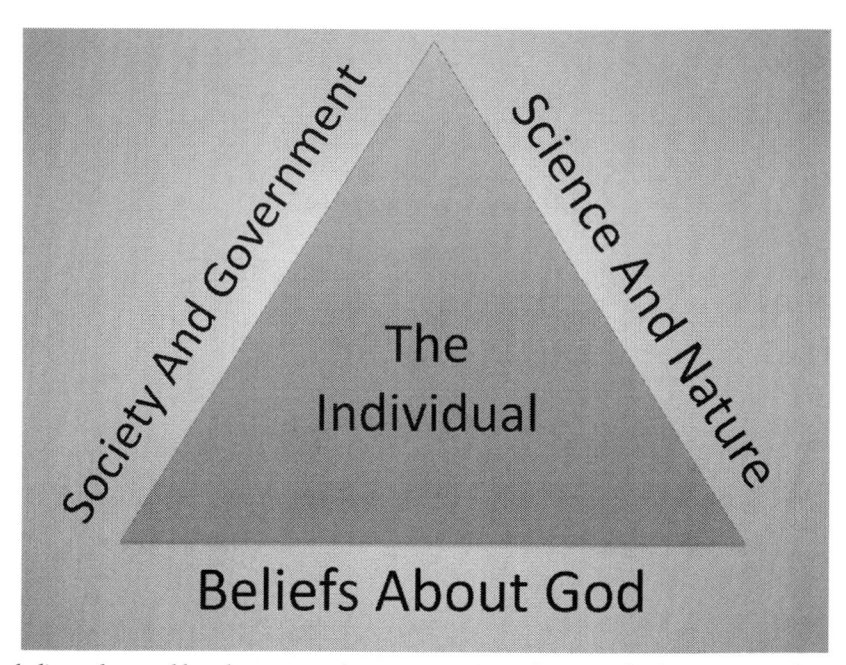

```
        Society And Government    Science And Nature
                    The Individual
                  Beliefs About God
```

believe the world and nature and our perception of it is really the strongest leg for most people. After all, how do Christians evangelize non-believers except through the testimony of what God has done in the real world? Human beings are decidedly practical, so our views about the natural world (science) largely determine our ideas about God and how we relate to the people around us.

The worldview of a believer looks like this. We believe in a created world and a Creator God, and those two aspects are so tightly intertwined that we could place either as the base. Those two aspects conspire to have some interesting impacts on our view of society and government. Because we believe in God's providence, we are less likely to see earthly government as an all-encompassing solution to human needs. We recognize man as a sinner, so we know the power of individuals, and therefore government, has to be restrained. We also have compassion for the needy among us, so we recognize the appropriate role of community and government in providing a safety net.

Removing America's historical belief in a created world transforms each individual into someone incompatible with the nation's founding and alienated from God. Without belief in a Creator, we lose our belief in a God who governs us spiritually. We become skeptical of faith and drift into secularism. Once we no longer rely on God's providence, our only hope is in collective action and the force of government. As men increasingly lose their moral compass, they rely on regulation and coercive law to control behavior because men can no longer govern themselves.

The two worldviews I described, either the believer or the humanist, illustrate worldviews in balance internally where each aspect of the worldview logically relates to the others. If only people were so reasonable! In reality, worldviews get convoluted and conflicted. For example, a person may be born and raised in a Christian home and may love church, but what happens if that person comes to love biology and comes under the teaching of an evolutionist who "explains" that living things develop naturally without a Creator? The result is a Christian believer spiritually and a humanist scientifically with a corollary tension between the person's spiritual and scientific beliefs. Those beliefs can coexist for years, but the tension between them is always there. His science tells him there is no creator, and his Bible tells him his God is the creator. Which does he believe? Which does he water down? When such foundational beliefs are in conflict, something's got to give.

Is it better for someone with a conflicted worldview to continue that way or to resolve the conflict? In his book, How Should We Then Live, the late Dr. Francis Schaefer explains the dilemma of modern man. Modern man accommodates his spiritual beliefs by separating them from the sphere of reason, allowing him to never reconcile these worldview conflicts. The resulting disconnect between the spiritual and material aspects of worldview destroys modern man's ability to examine ideas critically. I have an atheist Facebook friend who hates government interference with individual freedom but also thinks government must do something about greedy corporations. Does he think the corporations aren't run by individuals? Who decides when an individual is made free and when another individual is restrained? If my atheist friend had a consistent worldview, he would rely on government regulation and accept as a given that individual freedom will be limited in order to protect the collective. It goes back to Thomas Jefferson's great quote. If rights don't come from God, they will be decided by majority vote and government will enforce majority decisions. Understand I'm not advocating his worldview. I'm just suggesting that if he tried to reconcile his conflicted beliefs, it might lead to him overturning his atheist worldview. That's my prayer for the man.

The importance of understanding worldview is to get your worldview consistent so that you can function effectively in the real world. If you are a Bible-believer, God is identified consistently as the creator of all things. You will feel bad and behave irrationally if you reject that central truth. And if you are a believer in God and a created world governed by God, you need to relate to other people and human government in ways that flow from your worldview. Here are some ideas that flow from a believer's worldview:

- Individual human life is precious and inalienable rights come from God.
- Each person is responsible for his own welfare.
- Family is the essential building block of society.
- The weak and poor should be protected.
- Individuals given power should be restrained.

There is also such a thing as a consistent humanist worldview which looks something like this:

- Human rights are determined by the collective and are changeable.
- Society is responsible for individual welfare.
- The village is more important than the traditional family.
- Society should care for the weak and poor.
- The best and brightest should have control over planning society.

Although I'm not an advocate of humanism, I believe there would be less confusion if the two camps, believers and humanists, applied their worldviews consistently. It may even lead to individuals re-examining why they believe what they believe and reconsidering their worldview identification. Reconsidering worldview is what happens when a believer successfully disciples former non-believers.

In the next section we'll talk more about what fruits come from each of these worldviews.

What Effects Come From Worldviews?

So now that we know what we mean by "worldview", what difference does it make? The writer of Proverbs inspired by the Spirit recorded, "As a man thinketh, so is he." What we think about the world spills out in our actions and produces fruit. Let's then consider what each worldview produces.

The Fruit of Humanism

I believe you know this, for much has been written in books and related through the news and entertainment media about the negative effects of rejecting God. I certainly don't want to simply rehash a lot of bad news, so let me summarize the results of the humanist worldview and then touch on what I will call the unintended consequences. The term "humanist" came into vogue because atheists didn't want to be defined by what they don't believe in. Nevertheless, rejection of God is at the heart of the worldview. If there is no Creator God, then there can be no creation; so belief in material evolution is pretty much mandatory. In this sense, humanism has a very straight trajectory capturing the humanist into certain inescapable conclusions. Where a believer in God can consider evolution or creation, the humanist doesn't have a choice.

Thinking back on our worldview illustration as a triangle with three sides, the third side is how the humanist relates to people and government. This is where humanism breaks down as a practical philosophy because it has no basis for values and morality other than what individuals choose for themselves. Just as we learn in evolutionary biology that an organism's only goal is to survive and reproduce, a humanist's goal in his life among other people is to protect his self-interest. Because there is no authority higher than man, all a man can depend on is that every man is in it for themselves. Put simply, there is no-one you can trust because there is no transcendent standard for values or behavior. As a result of this inherent distrust implicit in humanism, humanists tend to favor government as a means to mediate activity among people. Since he trusts nobody, there must be legally binding regulations and controls over every area of human commerce. How else can the individual be protected?

What do I mean by the unintended consequences of humanism? Most humanists haven't thought things through. Most of my humanist friends are social liberals who distrust standards that are imposed either by law or religious morality. Nevertheless, without an imposed religious morality, individual liberty deteriorates into license and lawlessness. The solution to lawlessness is for society to pass laws through government which necessarily restricts individual freedom in arbitrary ways. This is the problem that every socialist, communist, or totalitarian system has produced...an oppressive destruction of individual freedom that is really in conflict with the original intent of free individuals. In wanting to be free from God, the humanist individual becomes enslaved first to the majority, but ultimately to the elite that was empowered by the majority.

Another unintended consequence of humanism is the suppression of the concept of the soul that sets mankind apart from the animals. What is love to a humanist? The humanist "knows" that the attraction between a man and a woman is an evolved response to assure reproduction and the continuation of the species. Evolutionary biologists explain the chemical and hormonal interactions that make attraction happen. If humanists really thought it through, they would conclude that romantic love is an illusion and not a bond that transcends mere biology. Why should a potential mate take seriously the proclamations of love from a humanist? And who would want to live, as the song goes, in a world without love?

What kind of man is a man who discards the Ten Commandments simply because they are the product of religious thinking? Is he against stealing or is he simply against getting caught? Does he feel honor-bound to tell the truth, or does he see lying as a useful strategy to further his own purposes. During the Christmas season, we often watch the movie, "It's A Wonderful Life", starring the great Jimmy Stewart. The hero of the story is given the chance to see what his community would be like if he had never lived, and he learns that the absence of his moral and ethical presence resulted in the advance of evil. What would the world be like if God never lived? Of course, I believe it wouldn't be here without a Creator; but if it could be here, it would be a place where every man did what seemed right in his own eyes. There would be no labels of good or evil, but rest assured that evil would abound.

The Fruit of A Biblical Worldview

A consistent Biblical worldview looks like this. There is a God who governs the affairs of mankind, and this God created all things. God inspired men to record the truth in the series of historical writings we now call the Bible. Since God created the universe and all that's in it, the Bible is authoritative regarding our origins, the course of history, the nature of man, and the promises of God. We can therefore use Scripture to determine how we should live individually and how we should govern collectively. There is so much that can be said about the consequences of believing God, but I'm going to focus here primarily on how belief relates to the third leg of our worldview triangle, relationship to people and society.

The Bible emphasizes individual responsibility. Perhaps this is why secular governments undermine individual initiative by promoting programs to take care of us. Taking care of the helpless sounds very "Christian", but government wants to classify too many of us as "helpless" so that we will accept dependency. Scripture makes it clear that anyone who is capable of helping themselves should be left to helping themselves. Paul writes in 1 Timothy 5 to "honor widows who are truly widows." The suggestion he makes is that younger women who find themselves single can work for a living or re-marry and that only the widows without options should receive assistance. Paul also writes in 2 Thessalonians 3 to have nothing to do with freeloaders. He continues, "We showed you how to pull your weight when we were with you, so get on with it. We didn't sit around on our hands and expect others to take care of us." The Bible isn't callous toward the truly helpless, but the Biblical worldview challenges and empowers every individual to take care of his own individual needs. Putting the principle in a political context, government should not promote an entitlement society and Biblical believers should not feel "un-Christian" if we reject the idea of handouts.

The family unit of father, mother, and children is the building block of society. Much has been written about the war on the traditional family in America primarily through the institution of marriage. Can two men be married? Can two women be married? Can marriage be more than two people? Can marriage have a specified term in years rather than "until death do you part?" It really takes a humanist to be confused regarding definitions most of us take for granted.

The Biblical alternative is clarity. "In the beginning God made them male and female" is not poetry. It is definition. Only real marriage produces new people through birth and childhood. All alternatives result in extinction. Biblical marriage provides the mechanism to raise children in the knowledge of the Lord to become mature and productively responsible adults so they can continue the cycle to expand God's kingdom on earth. The traditional marriage is profoundly other-centric whereas the humanist view is inherently self-centered. This is true regardless of what one might wish philosophically. Traditional family gives life and a future.

These ideas of the individual and family are at the core of the Biblical idea of collective government. Biblical government rests on each person taking care of himself, even to the extent of seeking help first from family before considering public assistance. It's a vital principle for keeping government limited and affordable. Biblical government also recognizes that men are prone to sin and will try to freeload if not raised according to Biblical teachings. Therefore, rather than excluding God from the public sphere, it is in the interest of the people to encourage the Biblical worldview.

What are the fruits then of a Biblical worldview? They would include stable marriages, children raised to be competent members of society, virtuous citizens living according to God's commandments, and government that protects citizens from crime and abuse while also limiting the power of corruption. Isn't that the kind of government we wish we had in the United States? Humanists may wish for something like this, but only God can deliver.

Conflicted worldview

Although both humanism and belief in God produce discernible fruit, there is also the more subtle result produced by a worldview in conflict or compromise. A conflicted Christian worldview produces strange fruit or unproductive fruit. President Barack Obama, who has called himself a Christian, wrote the following in "The Audacity Of Hope", regarding the United States Constitution, "Implicit in the Constitution's structure, in the idea of ordered liberty, was a rejection of absolute truth, the infallibility of any idea or ideology or theology or 'ism'..." If we take President Obama's testimony as a Christian to be true, then his apparent rejection of absolute truth is decidedly at odds with God's claims in the Bible. The President is part of a long humanist academic tradition that studies much but knows little. It's a tradition that rejects absolute truth and forces academics to re-evaluate even something as authoritative as a founding document into a plastic medium to facilitate interpretation and change.

This conflictedness of modern Christians has been a great challenge in developing CreationXpo as a Biblical worldview center because so many Christians mix humanist ideas into the way they look at reality. Yes, I believe that God created the world, but surely those dinosaurs lived millions of years ago. Yes, I believe in the Bible, but that story about Noah and the animals must be myth. Yes, it says that God created the first man and woman, but couldn't that mean Adam and Eve evolved from a pre-human species and the Bible is merely simplifying the story. Yes, I believe in personal responsibility and families helping their own, but shouldn't government extend unemployment benefits so an unemployed contractor shouldn't have to take a job at Lowes? So much conflict, so much confusion.

Of course the classic conflict in my creation science emphasis is the compromise of Bible believers with evolution. I hesitated to relate the following example because I was unsure how to make the right point, rather than just a superficial one. Dr. Gerald Schroeder is a Jewish physicist who believes in and teaches Old Testament doctrine. Nevertheless, he places more credence in mainstream cosmology than the book of Genesis. He is a Bible-believer who doesn't quite believe the Bible.

Gerald Schroeder rationalizes his preference for a Big Bang understanding of origins by attempting to revise the intent of Genesis. He does so by citing evidence from before the modern scientific age that Biblical Scholars rejected a historical understanding of the first chapters of Genesis and that, therefore, we shouldn't expect Genesis to be historically accurate. Essentially, the Bible is true but our understanding is not. Here is why Gerald Schroeder's argument should be rejected as representing a Biblical worldview:

- His basic premise is false, and he himself proves it. There is no time after the fall of Adam when mankind did not reject the truth claims of God. Schroeder offers us a little anecdote about the state of science in 1959 when most scientists accepted the ancient earth claims of Aristotle from

2400 years past. Then he jumps to Talmudic authorities who lived only 1500 years ago and claims that they wouldn't have been corrupted, confused, or misled by modern science. How foolish! Those scholars would certainly have known about Aristotle and would have "known" the secular assertion that the universe was infinitely old. They would have been influenced then to try to reconcile their understanding of the Bible with the popular notion of an eternal cosmos. They were as deluded as any modern unregenerate man.

- The oldest and least corrupted Biblical beliefs can clearly be seen in even older traditions. The almost universal adoption of the work week of seven days is our best evidence of man's earliest understanding of Genesis. The week has no astronomical or otherwise scientific origin, but only a Biblical origin; and its derivation clearly points to the seven days of creation as a contiguous, integrated period of time instead of one that can be dissected into pre and post Adam. Exodus 20:11 emphasizes the point by recording, "For in six days the Lord made heaven and earth, the sea, and all that is in them, and rested on the seventh day. Therefore the Lord blessed the Sabbath day and made it holy." Deciding that the first 6 days are qualitatively different from the 7th day is an interpretive stretch that seems to be inherently un-Biblical.

- Why would a Christian give any credence to ancient Talmudic scholarship? These were men who merged their fallible understanding of the Old Testament with Jewish tradition. These were men with unregenerate minds who had rejected Jesus Christ and lacked our access to enlightenment and edification through the Holy Spirit. These are the kind of people Jesus called "blind guides". Furthermore we are explicitly warned in the New Testament not to be misled by the traditions of men. Jesus' words are recorded in Mark 7:8, "Neglecting the commandment of God, you hold to the traditions of men." The traditions of men is what the Talmud is about.

- Schroeder's argument is a "foot in the door" argument rather than a complete reconciliation of the Bible and Science. Even if we allowed the universe to be billions of years old and reliable history begins with Adam as Schroeder implies, most secular scientists would remain unsatisfied. They would insist that there was no world-wide flood of Noah and that the fossil record and the evidence of evolution predated human history. Most would say that Moses never lived and that David was a fictional monarch. Most reject the virgin birth of Christ or any acknowledgement that the Bible is authoritative. Therefore, Schroeder's reconciliation doesn't reconcile anything at all.

- Finally and perhaps most importantly, the inadequacy of Big Bang cosmology as it exists today is widely acknowledged by scientists and is therefore almost certainly a wrong understanding of the universe. I read a scientific article recently in which researchers suggest the universe is really a holographic projection of a reality different from the Big Bang model. Although it's a fringe idea (now), it reveals the lack of resolve that physicists have for the current understanding of the cosmos. But here is the issue for Bible believers. Why should we deviate from a straightforward understanding of Genesis in deference to a secular humanist theory that isn't even accepted universally be secular humanists?

The old earth argument is at war with Christianity, and nobody knows this better than atheists. Harvard professor Ernst Mayhr observed "The revolution (against Christianity) began when it became obvious the earth was ancient...this was the snowball that started the whole avalanche." I truly sympathize with old-earth Christians because I know their heart is to find a rational way out of the apparent conflict between science and faith in a way that also honors God. But why try to integrate unsubstantiated humanist theories? Why are Christians so easily diverted from what the Bible says? Perhaps it has something to do with the social nature of people and how worldviews come about.

How Does Worldview Come About?

As I was planning this chapter on worldviews, I put together a list of questions that I thought someone would ask. They'd want to know what a worldview is, which ones exist, etc. "How a worldview gets started" seemed like a natural question, but that question could turn very technical. I could see myself scouring through volumes of research by credentialed psychologists, trying to isolate issues of nature or nurture to explain why people believe what they do. Actually, I can't see me doing that. I'm just going to give you my gut impressions. The two great drivers of worldview are association and revelation.

Association

It's pretty intuitive that most of us receive our initial values from association with our parents. The Bible teaches believers to "raise up a child in the way he should go, and he will not depart from it." Conversely, many non-believers suggest that children should be allowed to make up their own minds. Although that sounds liberating, it really conveys the "value" that nothing matters enough for the parent to instruct a child, so the child is actually indoctrinated in humanism by experiencing what other people think. As they grow to adulthood, children tend to reinforce the values established in them by choosing to associate with like-minded people. Believers associate with believers and non-believers with non-believers, and yes I am oversimplifying but nevertheless conveying a broad truth nevertheless. The associations we enter into are powerful amplifiers of our separate worldviews.

My friend Michael is a Christian missionary who spent time witnessing to Muslims in the Middle East. Witnessing to Muslims is much more than explaining doctrine or appealing to an individual's need for grace to overcome sin. After all, most people, including Muslims, have feelings of unworthiness in comparison to any god. But the big problem in winning converts to Christianity is that people in the Middle East are so communal, unlike Americans who are strong individualists. Family and community are such powerful cultural influences in the Middle East that most individuals won't consider a change in faith that would alienate them from their community. A Muslim converting to Christianity breaks all ties with family and friends and may even face immediate persecution. However, rarely is the persecution necessary, since the psychological threat of ostracism is so traumatic.

In America, the closest thing to this is our liberal universities where humanism is the dominant culture. The reason that universities are so dominated by liberalism and atheism is that university employees are members of an isolated and closed community. If all of your friends express liberal humanist views, there is pressure to join in. By pressure I mean the human need to belong and cooperate, although overt opposition can take place if someone deviates from "acceptable" beliefs. Ben Stein did a great job in *No Intelligence Allowed* to highlight how researchers who deviate from evolution can lose position, tenure, and reputations. It is not that university people are "evil". Their society is just so insular that they can't imagine different ways of thinking as being intellectually legitimate. It's that old "one of us is crazy" mentality, and it must be you. We can't have crazy people teaching at the university!

Revelation

The factor other than our associations that affects worldview is the new information that comes our way as we journey through life. We humans are learning creatures with both an intellectual and spiritual nature. Although our adult worldview my be greatly influenced by our upbringing, new information coming our way refines and even challenges the way we were raised. We'll talk more about this idea of revelation in the next section because it especially relates to changing worldview.

Can A Worldview Change?

Our associations want to filter out information in conflict with our worldview, so the challenge to anyone who wants to affect worldview is figuring out how to break through the associations. But the challenge isn't just about affecting other people. We should challenge ourselves to remain open to learning. As a Christian, I'm not interested in changing my service to the Lord, but I am always interested in perfecting my understanding of how to serve Him. We need to keep evaluating the details of our worldview to ensure that the details are aligned with principles. Otherwise we will find ourselves having an internal conflict.

Revelation and Change

Let me tell you about a friend I'll call "Edith". Edith grew up in a marginally Christian home and went through the typical rebellion as a young adult. She would come to consider herself proudly as a free spirit and subsequently fell in love with her soul mate. When Edith had a son and faced the daunting prospect of teaching and disciplining her child, she began to re-evaluate the need for greater structure in her lifestyle and worldview. Edith recommitted herself to Christ.

But not so fast. Edith still loved her "free spirit" persona. She considered herself fun and impetuous and loving to others. Christian doctrine seemed all too constraining. She had a cousin who announced he was gay, and Edith found herself trying to integrate her renewed walk with God with her feelings of love and compassion for the boy. Edith knew that homosexuality was "wrong", but so was judging others. And for that matter, don't we live under grace and not works? And her nephew claimed he was born that way, so isn't his sexual identity partly God's doing? Edith decided that endorsing and supporting her nephew's gay lifestyle was the Christian thing to do. Here is what she wrote:

> *"I have changed my beliefs some. I have known too many children that we have known were gay from the time they were little kids to believe its a choice. I support gay marriage and it was very hard for me to come to that because of my religious beliefs. What really changed my mind was that we have a cousin who fell in love, and I think those two fellas should be together (they are far happier than most heterosexual couples I know!), So last month Alex married his boyfriend and I support them because they belong together. And it's my RIGHT to support them."*

Ultimately all of Edith's self-talk about her gay nephew was centered on how she felt about it rather than God's perspective. Nevertheless, The conflict between Godliness and her free-spirit feelings rooted in Humanism remains an unresolved stress.

What should a Biblical thinker believe? I learned about Edith's journey through social media, and came to care about Edith because I sense the love she has both for God and for people. Maybe that's why it's so sad to me that this dear follower of Christ hasn't discovered God's heart for her nephew. The issue of Edith's nephew is not just making the sinner comfortable in his sin. The goal should not be so the young man can feel less judged or more normal. God's heart is for the sinner, Edith's nephew and me and you, to be saved from sin. God's heart is for repentance and restoration. My prayer for Edith is that she not keep one foot in humanism and the other in the Kingdom, but learn to see every issue through the Lord's eyes. My prayer also is that this new revelation leads Edith to straighten out her worldview and become comfortable in it.

How does worldview change? You challenge the inconsistencies. You restore an understanding of the most foundational principles. You bring out the tension between the details and the principles and let the individual resolve them. If you can also get the individual away from the associations that protect their worldview, the person becomes more open to change. Why will the individual want to resolve conflicts? They have to in order to have inner peace, and that's a powerful motivator.

Is Revelation Just Information?

What I mean by "revelation" isn't necessarily spiritual. I merely mean that all the information coming to each of us affords the opportunity for truth to become revealed. We in fact can be agents of revelation to the people we meet by engaging with them in the world of ideas. Remember our worldview illustration as a triangle with three aspects? Each side of the triangle is rich in information, but it's misleading to show the sides as equal in impact. Many people today are working on the political aspect of worldview, but all they're creating is unresolved argument. The leg of government is the weakest of the three sides of our worldview triangle. Science and faith more strongly determine our view of government than any purely political detail. As long as a growing segment of America's population rejects the providence of God, they will be unreceptive to the idea of limited government because, in their view, government is the only source of provision and safety. They are wrong, but they are behaving in a manner consistent with their worldview.

To effect real change, we need to work on all three aspects of America's worldview simultaneously. That's why this isn't just a book about politics or just about science or just about faith. We need to see worldview in totality where all three sides work together in unison.

Is A Biblical Worldview Viable?

> *If therefore there is any encouragement in Christ, if there is any consolation in love, if there is any fellowship of the Spirit, if any affection and compassion, make my joy complete by being of the same mind, maintaining the same love, united in spirit, intent on one purpose. – Philippians 2:1-2*

It's a tribute to the power of the Gospel that people indoctrinated in materialistic evolution have continued to accept Christ as Lord and Savior. That being said, science from a humanist worldview continues to be a major stumbling block keeping people from even considering the Gospel. For that reason, the proper understanding of scientific knowledge has become foundational to a Biblical worldview. The Bible begins with Genesis describing the creation of the universe, the Earth, and Man; and no successful Biblical worldview can deny the central truth of creation. Therefore, for a Biblical worldview to be credible and accepted, it must be based on sound, rational thinking.

The Scientific Method

The scientific method describes a way of thinking that can be applied to any area of thought, even the question of God or no God. Furthermore, the scientific method is the perfect style of thought to address people held captive by humanistic ideas because the method emphasizes observation and reason, factors which humanists value. However, where orthodox humanists limit observation to materialistic evidences, we include the testimony of Scripture in our arsenal of observations and facts. We can rationalize the inclusion of history because all science-based knowledge is the accumulation of learning from previous generations to our own.

With that in mind, let's consider how the scientific method works to distinguish truth from merely possibilities. The simple version looks something like this:

1. Observe some aspect of the universe.
2. Invent a tentative description, called a hypothesis, that is consistent with what you have observed.

3. Use the hypothesis to make predictions.
4. Test those predictions by experiments or further observations and modify the hypothesis in light of your results.
5. Repeat steps 3 and 4 until there are no discrepancies between theory and experiment and/or observations.

The concept of falsification is an important corollary to the scientific method whose purpose is to define what kinds of ideas can really be considered scientific. Ironically, in order to be considered scientific, it must be possible to disprove it. That means the scientific method can not be used to evaluate feelings and emotions or fervently held beliefs. A theory has to be fact-based, and any observation that contradicts a theory should technically indicate the theory is false.

Why should we consider using the scientific method? It has some clear advantages over other ways of considering a problem. It lets us test our ideas so we can feel more sure of our conclusions. It's very liberating. We can be surer of ourselves because it is not necessary to imagine or guess. It helps us avoid the philosophical bias to which we all succumb from time to time.

Unfortunately it's not always so easy. After all, scientists are people; they have a worldview bias just like normal people. To make matters worse, scientists are part of an establishment that tends to force individuals to conform. Every scientist's ideas relate to the combined ideas of the collective. It's a team effort, so it's hard to be a maverick even if the evidence demands it. Then when it comes to a subject like the reconstruction of past events, which is largely philosophical, it's even easier to be influenced by peer pressure.

To understand this better, let's consider a case study involving the origin of the universe. Humanists believe that the universe is self-existing rather than created. The popular name for the humanist theory of cosmology is the Big Bang. It rests on the belief that matter and energy and the laws of physics alone account for the origin and continuation of the universe. However, scientists observe that there is not enough matter to allow structures like galaxies to form and maintain themselves. This shortage of matter and energy is not just a problem for Big Bang cosmology, it is an inherent conclusion of the mathematics of the theory. If there isn't enough matter and energy, the theory has been FALSIFIED. Nevertheless, Big Bang cosmology explains so many of the observations astronomers have accumulated, and their humanist bias requires a materialist explanation. Letting go of the Big Bang is like starting over, an admission that their conclusions are wrong. Rather than abandon the theory, advocates invent "dark matter" and "dark energy" to explain the missing matter. They propose that most of the universe is invisible.

The science establishment has another alternative available to them, one which they typically fail to exercise. They could begin to investigate a model that has more explanatory power. Creation theory predicts that physical matter and energy alone cannot explain the universe. The Bible expresses that God's invisible power maintains the universe, and invisible power is what observation suggests.

Does this prove creation and disprove material evolution? No, of course not. But it illustrates the true status of man's knowledge of origins. We simply don't have enough facts and experimental data to decide scientifically between humanist ideas and theistic ideas about science. The right thing to do is study both models.

The Advantage Of Revelation

Scientists begin with observation, but Biblical creationists have an advantage over humanists. We have a historical record called the Bible to guide our investigation. Think of it as a scientific cheat sheet. It provides us with the testimony of many generations of men and women who lived before us. The following chart is an overview of the humanist and creationist interpretations of science:

Humanist Material Evolution Model	Biblical Creation/Design Model
Interpretive, not purely scientific. Events happened in the past and cannot be observed or tested.	Interpretive, not purely scientific. Events happened in the past and cannot be observed or tested.

Assume a **creator does not exist** so everything must come about by natural processes.	A **Creator/Designer exists** who brought everything about.
Geology: Rock layers represent millions of years of history.	**Geology:** Rock layers represent deposition by catastrophic processes and are historically and chronologically inconclusive.
Extinction: Fossils represent intermediary stages of life.	**Extinction:** Fossils show diversity of life diminished by extinction.
Homology: Similarity between organisms show they are related by inheritance.	**Homology:** Similarity between organisms show they are related by common design.
Cosmology: Big Bang theory represents the mechanics of the beginning of the universe.	**Cosmology:** Biblical Genesis and other creation stories reflect a universal memory of a design beginning.
Biology: Genetic mutation and selection leads to the diversity of life.	**Biology:** Genetics is a designed information system allowing diversity within limits.
Information Theory: Complexity comes through random changes and recombinations.	**Information Theory:** Complexity is the product of a mind; the design of an intelligent creator.

You can see that both models address the same evidence, but they interpret the evidence differently. It isn't a science versus religion conflict. It is interpretation versus interpretation. Because the humanistic model has such a dominant position among scientists, the creation model hasn't had a fair hearing. In subsequent chapters we are going to discuss the major areas of science related to origins and review what the objective facts are, what the Bible says, and what the best creationist theories look like. Our purpose is not so much to prove creation as to show that Biblical theories in every area are scientifically reasonable and not a stumbling block to the Biblical worldview. Furthermore, our ultimate goal is to provide for Christians everywhere a united point of view regarding the world around them. Re-read the verse at the beginning of this section. We are called to be of the same mind. That is why the Biblical worldview is so important.

Before we move on, lets lay the groundwork for a reasonable Biblical worldview of the universe and Earth science. A compelling argument in our favor is that scientists agree the universe had a beginning. Both sides also recognize that the universe is rich in information, and that in human experience, information demands an intelligent cause. Materialism, the idea that the existence of the universe is simply the way matter and energy works, is incompatible with belief in an intelligent cause. We would also posit that evidence alone rarely reveals an accurate picture of something otherwise unseen. An eyewitness testimony or history is always more meaningful than mere evidence, and the Bible is that history from the beginning. Therefore, before we move on to science, we'll have to consider what the Bible really says.

CHAPTER 2

What The Bible Says

You say that I am a king. In fact, the reason I was born and came into the world is to testify to the truth. Everyone on the side of truth listens to me. – Jesus' words in John 18:37

The Problem of Biblical Interpretation

I Mentioned previously that Bible believers have the advantage of receiving a written revelation from the Creator. The tragedy of the modern church is that Bible-believers don't share a common understanding of what the Bible says, so the great tool God has given us of Biblical revelation isn't being used to full effect. This is no more evident than in Genesis where we have such interpretations as theistic evolution, the gap, day-age theory, progressive creation, prophetic-interpretive theory, and more. Most of these theories about Genesis' explanation of origins were developed to address the encroachment of modern humanist science a hundred years ago. Simply put, if secular geologists didn't claim the Earth was billions of years old, no reader of Genesis would suggest a multi-million year gap between the first two verses of genesis. Therefore, for purposes of this study, let's imagine that we don't believe what humanists say. Let's begin with a blank canvas from a pure beginning.

We will treat the Bible as we would any other book by taking the words to mean what they say. Christians have become too accustomed to interpreting the

Bible. Imagine that your little boy comes home from school with a test paper with a failing grade. You ask Johnny what happened, and he explains he had to answer ten questions based on a chapter in his textbook. "Why did you get eight out of the ten wrong?" you ask. Johnny explains, "They're not wrong; I just interpret the textbook differently than my teacher." The Bible isn't meant to mean whatever we interpret it to mean. God inspired a true meaning and meant it to be understood.

Nevertheless, some Christians will object; and I sympathize completely. They might say that the Bible is written poetically or that you have to understand the historical context and culture in order to interpret its meaning. They might also say that the writers of Scripture were scientifically naïve and simply didn't understand the true nature of the universe. That thinking seems to presuppose that the Bible is just an ordinary book written by primitive men and that it wasn't inspired by the Creator to be understandable to people of all ages and nations. Quite frankly, it's a humanist way of looking at Scripture. Although I am a scientific thinker and perceive the possibilities of interpretation and also acknowledge that we can learn by examining God's created world, I nevertheless am committed to an understanding of Earth history based on the clear meaning of Scripture. If you believe that the Bible can accommodate gaps or millions of years or guided evolution, I ask humbly that you suspend judgment and consider the model I am presenting. I intend to present clear and scientifically viable concepts that are consistent with a straightforward, non-interpretive reading of Genesis. Christians should not become divided over this because it is only science. Creationists of different sorts are never enemies nor do our fallible ideas about science jeopardize our relationship as brothers or our salvation. No need to get upset. It's only science.

Let me also make it clear that I don't claim to have the details of Biblical worldview perfectly accurate. Think of this work as a starting point applying scientifically credible concepts from a straightforward, non-interpretive understanding of Scripture.

Objections To Reading The Bible Plainly

Why do people choose to interpret the Bible? Clearly portions of Scripture demand that we figure out the meaning. The book of Revelation is the most noteworthy example. Understanding Revelation is complicated by the fact that many of the events it describes are prophesied for the future, so we don't have the actual event to measure it against. Add to that fact that prophetic writings tend to be like word pictures that tap into our imaginations and we end up with a vision of what it means but lots of loose ends in the details.

Genesis is very different because the events and processes have already taken place, and we should be able to find evidence of them. Unfortunately, many of the events described by Genesis are also one-time happenings and cosmic events on a scale we can't imagine. Since the truth of those events is hard to demonstrate, we're easily swayed by the criticisms of secular humanists. They say, "how can you get all the animals in the ark," and we look for a convenient explanation. "Maybe it didn't happen quite like it says" tends to be a very convenient escape. Oh but all those compromises and evasions do add up.

We also interpret Scripture because we've been taught to by well-meaning preachers who learned from other well-meaning preachers who sincerely tried to reconcile their understanding of the natural world with Genesis. The gap theory, the day age theory, theistic evolution, progressive creation, and other compromises have been propagated by Biblical teachers all trying to reconcile their understanding of creation with humanistic science. The common man who doesn't have time to research these things tends to accept the ideas of a respected teacher in the church.

Another reason some people deviate from a plain understanding of the Bible is they've never read it through and don't know what it really says. If you aren't confident in what Genesis says, you might easily be swayed by the criticism of an atheist who may even present the Bible wrongly as part of his argument.

The last reason I will give you is little more than "habit". Christianity is very fragmented into denominations and doctrines and schools of thought, and each of these has their own ideas about what is true. My own pastor describes the various churches as different flavors of Christianity like ice cream flavors with all of the flavors being good. What Pastor Jerry means is that the various styles of church allow for inclusiveness in accommodating different tastes regarding worship music, service schedules, preaching methods, and such. However, I can't help thinking that the way we Christians seek our favored outward style and segregate according to "flavor" reflects an underlying propensity for division in the deeper matters of doctrine and truth. Flavors are good, but they must be tempered with our commitment to the greater Christian community and the truth claims of God.

The Secular Seduction

Astrophysicist Neil deGrasse Tyson offered his advice about eight books every person should read. Because he's an outspoken atheist, I was intrigued by his choice of the Bible as #1 until I read his summary... "to learn that it's easier to be told by others what to think and believe than it is to think for yourself."

Although Neil deGrasse Tyson is a smart man and a well-educated one, his assertion is foolish. One of the keys of human civilization is that all of us are the product of the accumulated knowledge of all the people who came before us. Believers can add that we have the accumulated knowledge of the Spirit-filled saints who preceded us in life. All of these voices from the past testify to us what they learned in life. They tell us what to think. To deny this is to reject the greatest sources of knowledge we have and to replace it with whatever we make up in our own heads in our one individual life. DeGrasse Tyson does not really believe his own words because he would be happy if everyone accepted the accumulated knowledge of scientific humanists. He would recognize that society progresses through accumulated experience. What deGrasse Tyson is speaking against is the knowledge of God and the authority of God, and he is being deliberately deceptive.

Part of our struggle as believers is that we are easily influenced by people we want to admire, whether great scientists or performing artists or athletes. We can even see humanist thinkers as heroes in their particular area of expertise, and then we mistakenly accept their ideas in areas where they are ignorant. Neil deGrasse Tyson is a fine scientist and an entertaining advocate for scientific thinking and an educated person, but many people with expertise in their area of knowledge are fools when it comes to understanding the things of God. So let's not let ourselves get sucked in by educated fools.

All of the reasons we have for not accepting the plain meaning of Scripture and re-interpreting have a similar basis. People are more easily swayed by Man (humanism) than they are by God. They don't have to deal with God much, but they do have to cope with their atheist friend.

Why Read The Bible Plainly?

> *"And I saw another angel fly in the midst of heaven, having the everlasting gospel to preach unto them that dwell on the earth, and to every nation and kindred and tongue and people, saying with a loud voice, fear God, and give glory to him; for the hour of his judgment is come, and worship him that made heaven and earth and the sea and the fountains of waters."*

The passage is of course from Revelation, the book of the Bible farthest removed from Genesis, yet persistently proclaiming the importance of God's role and position as the Creator of all things. Because he is the Creator, God makes the rules and his description of the world and his rules is central to understanding the Biblical worldview and our obligation as Christians governed by it. His book of Genesis is all we have to describe God's acts of creation. It should be no surprise to us then that the world system is at war with Genesis. What is surprising though is that the church has no unified response because of internal divisions over the very nature of truth in Scripture.

There is a principle in reasoning referred to as Ockham's Razor (from William of Ockham). It is a principle of parsimony, economy, or succinctness used in logic and problem-solving. It states that among competing hypotheses, the hypothesis with the fewest assumptions should be selected. The razor principle states that one should use the simplest theories until the evidence requires that simplicity be traded for complex theories having greater explanatory power. In other words, the simplest explanation should be your starting point. As a mature Christian, I applied Ockham's Razor to Genesis and decided to take Genesis to mean what the words express, that God created everything in short order and culminated his creative acts with the making of the first man. The rest of Scripture is laced with genealogies which establish mathematically that man has only been around a few thousand years. As a scientific investigator, I used this understanding of Genesis as an anchor to generate a scientific model. Through my investigations, I never encountered reasons to abandon the simplicity of the straightforward, non-interpretive understanding of the words of Genesis.

A scientific purist may object that I am merely inventing science to support my preconceived ideas regarding the nature of the world, but I would point out that is what all scientists do. An atheistic scientist proceeds from the assumption that there is no creator. Having no revelational anchor point, he is limited only by his imagination. Observing a created universe, he imagines how it might have come about without cause or direction and envisions nothing springing into everything through a process popularized as the Big Bang. He invents schools of physics that describe how it might have happened and writes mathematical formulas within that framework. In spite of all the trappings of science, he despairs that he can ever know whether what he imagines is true, because the hypothesis can never be tested and there is no anchor point to rely on. He is adrift.

Recently I have been pondering where the church universal stands regarding science and the Bible, and I fear the church is also adrift with no consensus regarding our roots and responsibilities. Christians have been wooed by their own learning experiences often based on atheistic models of science to reinterpret Genesis as either containing an unrevealed gap or being allegorical, prophetic, and poetical. In other words, Genesis must not mean what it says because the plain meaning is in conflict with their secular learning. In developing and maintaining a Christian worldview center, I don't know what to do with that. Christians who believe such things are like the atheists in being regulated only by their imaginations. As believers, we try not to step on each other's feelings or hurt each other, and that's not my intent. I just don't know how to build a worldview model on such a subjective foundation as a Genesis that might mean many things. More importantly, we Christians have just stopped talking about it. Lacking authority in Genesis even among ourselves, we'd just as soon not discuss it with lost people because we feel just as lost as they are. It's very sad.

So what can I do to present Christian truth when Christians are so divided over what is true? I am applying Ockham's Razor. I have purposed myself to pursue the straightest path in understanding the Creator's works. I believe that God has spoken so as to be understood by men. It is not God's way to be confusing or mysterious or misleading. Deuteronomy 30:11-14 is the cry of God's heart regarding his desire to communicate with us:

> *"You know God's laws and it isn't impossible to obey them. His commandments aren't in heaven so you might say 'how can we know them because they're in heaven, and no one can go get them and explain them to us.' And you can't say 'they are across the sea so we can't see them. No, you know my commands by heart."*

An essential truth of Christianity is that God wants to communicate with us. He wants relationship and fellowship and respect. In order for this to be true, God's word must be intuitively understandable, straightly written, and intended for our comprehension. God's Word isn't an incomprehensible puzzle open to interpretation. It's meaning is clear. You don't need to be adrift.

The Bible Story

The following is a summary of the basic story of the Bible. It's hard to create a summary because there isn't anything in the Bible that shouldn't be there. However, it's useful to isolate just the basic story line for the sake of clarity.

Creation

We start in the beginning with God creating the heavens and the earth and everything in them in six days. The creation week culminates in God making man in His own image, and Adam and Eve enjoyed close fellowship with God in a special reserve called Eden. God pronounced His creation to be good and rested on the seventh day.

The Fall

God gave the man and woman the one requirement not to eat the fruit of the Tree of the Knowledge of Good and Evil or they would die. Adam and Eve failed their only test. A serpent (Satan) manipulated Adam and Eve to eat the fruit by insinuating that God was withholding knowledge. Humanity fell from a position of grace when God put a curse on the creation and expelled Adam and Eve from Eden.

The Flood Judgment

People filled the earth for centuries spiritually separated from their Creator, so God decided to intervene. A man named Noah pleased God, so God told Noah to build an ark to save his family and representative animals from a flood which God sent to cover the whole earth. After the flood, Noah built an altar and thanked God, and the descendents of Noah began to fill the earth again. The story of Babel describes prideful men working to establish a name for themselves. God confused their languages and scattered them, thus forming the nations of the earth.

God's Chosen People

A man named Abraham was chosen to father a people that would worship God and testify to the rest of the world. Abraham became the patriarch of both the Judeo-Christian and Islamic religions. God promised Abraham that he would be the father of more people than the stars in the sky, but neither he nor his wife Sarah waited on God's Timing. Abraham had a son with Sarah's maidservant who subsequently fathered the Arab people. But this son Ishmael was not the son that God promised. Fourteen years later, Sarah bore their promised son, Isaac.

Isaac had two sons, Esau and Jacob. God gave Jacob a new name, Israel. Jacob had twelve sons whose families formed the twelve tribes of Israel. Jacob had a favorite son, Joseph, who made the other sons jealous. They sold him as a slave to some men on their way to Egypt, which eventually led to the people of Israel moving to Egypt because of famine.

Moses And The Exodus

During the 430 years that the Israelites were in Egypt, they became slaves to the Egyptians. Moses was born to Israelite slaves but he was raised as a son of Pharaoh. When Moses was older, he murdered an Egyptian while defending one of the Israelite slaves and fled into the desert. After another 40 years, God spoke to him from a burning bush and instructed him to go back to Egypt and lead the Israelites out. Moses contended with Pharaoh until God miraculously delivered his people from the Egyptians.

Moses and the Israelites wandered 40 years through the desert to Mt. Sinai where God gave them the Ten Commandments. God had them build a portable Tabernacle as a place to worship Him during their travels.

Establishment Of The Law

God gave the Israelites instructions on worship and on offerings and sacrifices for sins. The Jewish laws were very detailed and complicated, but Jesus would eventually say that all the law could be reduced to, "Love God with all of your heart, soul, mind and strength," and, "Love your neighbor as yourself." All of the other commands are based on these two.

The Nation Of Israel

For three hundred years, the Israelites were led by spiritual guides called judges. When neighboring nations attacked the Israelites, they would cry to God for help, and God would raise up a judge to lead them. The last judge was Samuel. The Israelites asked Samuel to let them have a king like the other nations. God chose Saul as the first king, but he didn't obey God. So God chose David as king because David had a heart that followed God.

Shortly thereafter, the nation of Israel became divided and the new nations of Judah and Israel had good, Godly kings and also bad kings. God sent prophets to warn the nations to return to honor God, but they didn't repent. So, God sent the Assyrians to conquer Israel and take them away to foreign lands. Finally, God sent the Babylonians to conquer Judah and take most of the people to Babylon. These were the years of captivity.

After 70 years, God allowed many of the Jews to return to the Promised Land where they rebuilt the temple and the city walls of Jerusalem. For four hundred years, there were no prophets or messages from God. The Jews were conquered by the Greeks, then by the Romans. They were ruled by foreign kings. But God never forgot his promise to David that one of his descendents would rule over the nation. God had not forgotten his promise to Adam and Eve that one of their descendants would crush the power of sin.

Jesus

Jesus was born in a stable to a poor couple named Mary and Joseph who were both descendants of David. His name means "God saves." Angels foretold that he would be born the Son of God. Angels announced that he was born a Savior, Christ the Lord.

When Jesus was about thirty years old, he was baptized by John and began his public ministry. He chose twelve disciples to be apostles. For three years, they traveled around the Promised Land. Jesus healed the sick, raised the dead and cast out demons. He walked on water and even the wind and the waves obeyed him. He taught people about true and genuine righteousness, worship, prayer and service. His life is an example of humility, purity, friendliness, mercy and grace.

Many people followed Jesus, but the religious leaders hated him because he did not follow their man-made traditions. They arrested Jesus, but the only charge against him was that he claimed to be the Son of God. The religious leaders turned the hearts of the people against Jesus. He was nailed to a cross until he died and he was buried.

Early on Sunday morning, Jesus arose from the dead just as he had promised his disciples. For forty days, he appeared to them at different times and places. He told them to go into all of the world and spread the good news that he had conquered sin and death. Then Jesus ascended into Heaven. He is now with God the Father and intercedes for mankind. His death was the perfect sacrifice for every sin, from Adam and Eve to the end of time. His shed blood established a new covenant of salvation by grace, not works. His death and resurrection opened up the door to Heaven and eternal life for everyone who trusts in him.

The Church Age

At first, the believers were all Jews, but God's plan was to fulfill the original purpose of the Jews, to witness to the whole world. God sent Peter to preach to Gentiles at the house of Cornelius, a Roman soldier. He sent the apostle Paul through Cyprus and into Asia Minor to tell both Jews and Gentiles about Jesus. Many people believed and many churches were started. Later, Paul spread the good news about Jesus through Asia Minor and Greece. When Paul returned to Jerusalem, he was falsely accused by the Jews, and was sent to Rome for trial before Caesar. In spite of a shipwreck, Paul arrived in Rome and spent two years under house arrest. Apparently he was released but later arrested again and put to death.

Most of the New Testament related the formation of the Christian church throughout the Roman Empire. During the next millennium up until today, Christianity grew to represent the greatest number of the world's people compared to other religions or philosophies. Christianity has been a catalyst for the greatest explosion of learning, prosperity, and human liberty in history.

The End Times

The book of Revelation prophesies about the events that will lead up to the return of Jesus Christ. Then, all of the dead will be resurrected and judged according to their lives. All unrepentant sinners will be thrown into the lake of fire along with Satan and his demons. Everyone whose name is written in the Book of Life will enter into the New Jerusalem, the Holy City, where God dwells. There will be no death, sorrow, tears or anything evil. They will live forever in the presence of God.

There are various schools of thought regarding when the end times will arrive. Scripture reveals there will be a time when "men's hearts will grow cold" and faith will be diminished in the world. There will be wars and rumors of war culminating in a great tribulation and climactic conflict called Armageddon. Many Christians believe we are living at the start of the end times right now.

Future Prophesy And World Events

It would be wrong of me not to touch on the convergence of Biblical prophecy and current events, because these matters define what Christians believe about the unfolding of history. These are exciting times. We have seen the restoration of Jews to the land of Israel, an event that was foreseen by Scripture but seemed impossible just a few years before 1948 when it came to fruition. We have seen the rise of Israel's Islamic enemies to become a force in the world that also was not anticipated by secular policy makers. Most surprisingly, we have seen Israel become a hated nation in the world after several decades of being the sympathetic victims of Nazi destruction. I never would have thought that even America would become lukewarm in its support of Israel.

The newest source of amazement is that the United States, once a Christian nation, is experiencing an undercurrent of anti-Christian sentiment by a secular humanist minority that hates belief in God and sees that belief as an obstacle to homogenizing the world's people into a more compliant citizenry. Accompanying the anti-God trend is the growing sentiment for centralized political power to "protect" the people, to keep them safe, and to provide the paternal providence for which citizens once trusted God. Ironically, these same global secularists are doing the very things predicted in Scripture for the end times, a world-wide system that people can only participate in if they "take the mark" of subservience to authority. Several years ago, Biblical prophecy investigators were wondering why the United States seems to be missing from our understanding of the end times. We read about forces from the north attacking Israel and speculate that could mean Russia, but where is the greatest power from the west rushing to the defense of its ally, Israel? Little did we understand what we suspect now. The United States is in such precipitous decline that it will no longer be the moral world power to intervene in anyone's defense. America is being taken out spiritually, financially, and politically.

These are the events that define how most of the American church feels, and many find it depressing. However, it ought to be a source of confidence for Biblical thinkers. These events show that God was not taken by surprise. The Lord referred to many of them as the signs of the times, the death throws of the old system before His return. It is why having a Biblical worldview or perspective is so vital to the church, for we are not ignorant of what is happening. I am not suggesting that we merely be fatalistic in accepting what has been prophesied however. Our role as the Lord's servants is to warn everyone everywhere. I love the story of the watchman in Ezekiel 33 in which a key verse reads,

> "When I say to the wicked, Wicked man, you shall certainly die; and you don't speak to warn the wicked from his way, that wicked man shall die in his iniquity; but his blood will I require at your hand."

Each of us will be accountable if we see dangers and don't shout a warning.

CHAPTER 3

The Nature Of The Universe

What time is it? Forget for a moment that you are reading a book and consider the question. What time is it? If you're using a digital device, the time is probably displayed rather prominently, often at the top of the display. If you're reading paper and don't have your phone or tablet in view, you probably still have a clock on the wall somewhere. Even more importantly, you almost certainly have an intuitive idea of the time. Unless you're retired, you probably know what day it is and can guesstimate the hour. We are time-driven creatures, measuring the time to our next commitment, maybe dreading the time we have to go back to work, or counting the hours and minutes for work to end. We celebrate special times like birthdays and holidays and anniversaries. What is more regular and measurable and inevitable than the passage of time? Without time, we wouldn't know or appreciate that we are alive.

The Allure Of The Cosmos

Cosmology, astronomy, and the universe are subjects that blow our minds regarding time; and humanists use these topics to confuse our understanding. Humanist cosmologists introduce us to light years as a unit of measure of distance and claim they observe celestial objects billions of light years away. Then they assert that the speed of light is fixed and that light from distant objects has therefore traveled for billions of years. Many believers in God have been lured into acquiescence reasoning that God could use billions of years because He is outside of time. Unfortunately, your kids and grandkids won't see it that way. The dichotomy between thousands of years of Biblical history and billions of years cosmic history is intuitive to a child. The mature believer's ability to rationalize the dichotomy is lost on children. For better or worse, they see through it. That's why cosmology is such an important starting point in our defense of the Biblical model of science, and it's why we don't just jump on board with an ancient universe.

The universe embodies the entire creation. Its very name, meaning "one word", is theistic, describing how God spoke the universe into existence. Its alternate name, the cosmos, is equally revealing, derived from a Greek word meaning "orderly arrangement" with a secondary sense of "ornamentation, particularly of a woman." The universe has a special fascination for us. Looking into the night sky fills us with wonder like staring into the flame around a campfire. It represents the "big picture" of the creation providing a kind of framework for every other aspect of scientific investigation. Herein lies the problem.

According to Big Bang cosmology, the universe is the ultimate evidence for billions of years. Humanists and believers influenced by humanism see the universe as too vast for it to have been created. They also see planet Earth as too tiny to be of ultimate importance. These are naïve thoughts if you believe in an infinite God, but they are very influential concepts to very finite human beings. We are so familiar with our feelings of insignificance and so easily swayed by other people's opinions. However, the Big Bang theory isn't nearly as settled or even anti-God as most people imagine. It is often used as "proof" against creation but the Big Bang is about mechanics rather than cause. God's process of creation could have produced the same characteristics as a Big Bang Universe. The Big Bang is used as "proof" that the universe is billions of years old, but Einstein's physics indicates that time itself is a variable. Big Bang theory can produce an old or young universe. Does light take billions of years to reach earth? That's a nonsensical question if time is a variable. Were they really fast years or really slow years? Then again, physicist James Clerk Maxwell believed that light is nearly infinitely fast in deep space. Starlight may be reaching us in hours rather than millions or billions of years. If light speed is a variable, what distance is a light year and how does that relate to age?

The historical narrative of the Bible gives us many clues about the nature and creation of the universe. Because cosmology is abstract and theoretical, a historical framework is helpful. Consider this story. Two archaeologists of the future discover the ruins of the Lincoln Memorial in Washington, D.C. One archaeologist reasons that the structure is over 2,000 years old because the architecture is indicative of the classical Greek era. The second archaeologist looks at a history book and reads that the Lincoln Memorial was completed in 1922. Which scientist got it right? The one with a history book of course. This little story illustrates the limitations of science in regard to the past. Whatever theory you might piece together from mere evidence and artifacts will always lead to some degree of error, whereas an eye-witness account, if you can trust it, represents verified detail.

As we go through each area of science (universe, living things, geology), we will use this recurring theme. We will consider what scientists observe, attempting to strip away assumptions and inferences. Then we will consider the predominant secular theory about the subject. From there we'll proceed to what the Bible says as a historical, eye-witness reference. Finally, we will relate one or more credible Biblical alternatives to the humanist version. Although I am striving for truth, even with a historical reference we can never know or verify that we know what happened in the past in detail. What I can assure you is that you need not distrust God's Word because of scientific thinking. God invented everything we're talking about.

The Problem Of Physics

It's intimidating. It's theoretical. It's based on mathematics that looks like none of the math we learned in high school. It's been said that only a select few people in the world can speak knowledgably about theoretical physics, although many others speak as if they understand. Theoretical physics is the underpinning of modern cosmology and our understanding of the universe. Nevertheless, I find myself a little disinterested. I'm disinterested because it is very possible that most physicists don't understand anything at all. String theory, quantum theory, relativity, time dilation, multiple universes, etc. etc. Is light a wave or a particle? Do atoms really look like those neat mini solar systems we've seen in textbooks? Probably not. Is it true what one theorist published recently that the visible universe is merely a holographic projection of a completely different reality? Is the speed of light an absolute limit that will prevent us from trekking around the universe like Kirk and Spock? There's lots of stuff up for grabs in our understanding of the fundamental nature of the matter and energy we see as the visible universe. I simply have no confidence that physicists have it right. I wish I had the time (and talent) to investigate it myself, but I'm a museum guy...jack of all trades and master of none. Therefore let me admit I am mostly copping out in terms of any deep theoretical understanding of the universe. I'm going to concentrate on its physical characteristics. This is not to say that creationist cosmologies don't imply things about theoretical physics that we will touch on. Just don't look for detailed theoretical explanations.

What Scientists Observe

What scientists observe is a good place to start because it represents the plain facts without too much interpretation. What are the observations of scientists about the universe? It's big. Astronomers recently discovered the most distant object in the universe at 13 billion light years away. The vastness of the universe is both a testimony to God and a stumbling block. It's a testimony in that it speaks of the power and expansiveness of God. But why would God create something so big to support little old us?

The size of the universe is a stumbling block because the very laws of physics that God ordained seem to indicate the universe is billions of years old. If the universe is only thousands of years old as most theistic creationists believe, how can we see light from stars that are billions of light years distant? Creating light in transit isn't a good answer. If the light was created separate from its star, the light we see was never emitted by the star and the star is in a sense an illusion. That's inconsistent with our fervent belief that God embodies truth, that He is honest and trustworthy.

Another seemingly important observation of astronomers is that the light from distant objects is shifted toward the red end of the light spectrum. What causes this? We'll learn that the standard interpretation is that red shift means the universe is expanding, but that's an interpretation, not necessarily a correct interpretation. That means we can't even be sure the expanding universe is a true observation.

The interaction of gravity and matter is insufficient to explain the structure of the universe. Based on pure observational evidence, we don't know how stars form or why they become grouped by the millions in swirling galaxies. All we truly observe is their existence, not their origin. In addition to stars, we observe exotic objects like quasars and black holes. Do those objects suggest anything about the creation?

But it isn't just exotic or big objects that scientists observe. There is also the world of the very small where observation and theoretical speculation co-exist in an uneasy relationship. What is matter, for example? At the atomic level, matter is defined in terms of positive and negative charges - protons and electrons. The most basic element, hydrogen, is one proton and one electron. All the rest of the periodic table of elements builds upon multiples of balanced protons and electrons whose modular construction is reminiscent of the zeros and ones of computer programming language. For all of our knowledge of matter's simple design, we are unable to create a single complex atom from free protons and electrons because we haven't mastered the strong nuclear force that holds the components of atoms together. What we observe from atomic theory is that information is at the foundation of the universe. The universe is information-rich.

We are equally mystified by energy. What is light, for example? Light sometimes behaves like particles which we call photons, but light also exhibits properties of waves. We speculate that light sets the speed limit for the universe and that its speed is constant, but experimental evidence suggests otherwise. The nature of matter and energy determines our interpretation of the material universe, and there is much we need to learn.

This has been a summary of observations, but it's important to elaborate that cosmic observations are always on the edge of interpretation. Consider for example something as simple as measuring the distance to a star. We obviously can't send a rocket to a star stretching out a long tape measure, so how is distance measured? The only physical measurement we can use is parallax, which involves the idea of triangulation and trigonometry. According to one definition, stellar parallax is defined as the apparent change in position of a nearby star when observed from opposite sides of the earth's orbit-that is, at a six-month interval. Think of the parallax method as a giant triangle where the diameter of Earth's orbit is the base of the triangle and the other two sides of the triangle are lines of equal length to the star sited from Earth at opposite sides of its orbit around the Sun. Astronomers measure the slight angle at the end of the triangle in order to calculate the length of the triangle's two equal sides. Even though the distance from one side of Earth's orbit to the other is big (about two times 93 million miles), the distance to the nearest star is huge. The more distant the star, the smaller is its parallax angle. That means we can only use parallax to measure distance to the very nearest stars.

How then do astronomers measure the distance to extremely distant stars? This is where astronomy can get less than purely observational. Astronomers are forced to depend on measurement involving such things as apparent brightness to determine distance. Since there are considerable differences in the actual size and brightness of stars, astronomers make assumptions about the nature of each star to estimate their actual brightness before they can use apparent brightness to estimate distance. Although such ideas are logical, they're not purely observational in a tape measure sort of way. It's simply the best we can do until warp drive is invented.

I don't believe there is anything more that I would include as observation. The universe is big, it's in motion, and it's based on information. The other "facts" some people would include are really the result of a theoretical belief system. For example, a big bang cosmologist would assert that there must be dark matter because the universe needs more mass than we observe in order to fit big bang models. They would say that dark matter is therefore "observed" because it has to be there to support their theory.

The Standard Cosmology

How do humanistic scientists interpret what they observe? The Big Bang is the standard cosmological model of the universe whose primary assertion is that the universe has expanded into its current state from a primordial condition of enormous density and temperature. The standard theory suggests that all the matter and energy of the universe was once concentrated in one tiny point which cosmologists call a singularity. Some would even say that point was so concentrated that all the matter and energy came from nothing at all, which leads some critics of the Big Bang to mock the theory by pointing out the absurdity of everything coming from nothing all by itself. The theory goes on to say that the singularity suddenly expanded or inflated and that matter, energy, and time itself began during that initial inflation. Initially, all the universe's matter was composed of light elements like hydrogen and helium and the heavier elements were generated later. The red shift we see in stars represents the continuing expansion of all of space along with the objects contained in space.

Theoretical support for the Big Bang comes from mathematical models. These models show the Big Bang theory is consistent with the theory of general relativity and with the cosmological principle. The latter states that the properties of the universe should be independent of position or orientation. Some educators have used the surface of a balloon to illustrate space. As the balloon is inflated, every spot on the surface of the balloon moves farther away from every other spot on the balloon. If space is curved like the surface of a balloon, then there really is no center anywhere on that surface. Most cosmologists would say there is no center of the universe because of the cosmological principle. Wherever you are in the universe, just like the inflating balloon surface, every observable object is moving away from you. Observational evidence for the Big Bang includes analyses of the spectra of light from galaxies, which reveals a shift towards longer wavelengths proportional to each galaxy's distance in a relationship described by Hubble's law. Combined with the assumption that observers located anywhere in the universe would make similar observations, this suggests that space itself is expanding.

The next most important observational evidence was the discovery of cosmic microwave background radiation in 1964. This had been predicted as a relic from when the hot, ionized plasma of the early universe first cooled sufficiently to form neutral hydrogen. This discovery led to general acceptance among physicists that the Big Bang is the best model for the origin and evolution of the universe. A third important line of evidence is the relatively large proportion of light chemical elements in the universe. Big Bang theorists believe that heavier elements formed according to a process called nucleosynthesis over a long period of time from the initial light elements. Since light elements were the only elements created in the beginning, light elements predominating is a reasonable prediction of Big Bang theory.

If all of this sounds confusing, that's because it is. Scientists are not in complete agreement by any means about the Big Bang because the theory leaves considerable room for mathematical tweaking with profound possibilities. For example, some theorists claim that the singularity never existed. They say the universe is eternal with repetitive big bangs separated by billions of years of expansion and subsequent contraction. When we look at creationist cosmologies, we will see that one of them tweaks the big bang to have a center, and allow time dilation effects to define a young Earth in an ancient universe. At our current state of scientific knowledge, almost anything is possible in the context of the Big Bang.

What Scripture Says

Now that we have looked at observation and the standard cosmology that humanistic investigators have devised, let's look at what the Bible tells us about the universe. Biblical creationists often cite Exodus 20:11 as a proof text for the context of creation. It reads, "For in six days the Lord made the heavens and the earth, the sea and all that is in them, and rested on the seventh day; therefore the Lord blessed the Sabbath day and made it holy." Exodus 20:11 is important because it effectively refutes any intellectual wavering in our understanding of Genesis, because there is no room left for gaps or long evolutionary processes or distinctions between the time God took to make the universe separate from the creation of Adam and Eve. But there is more to this than just verse 11. Exodus 20 is where we have the first appearance of the Ten Commandments, the heart of the moral teaching of Scripture, and in it God makes it clear that He is intolerant of humanistic ideas about creation. Exodus 20:3-6 reads, "You shall have no other gods before me. You shall not make for yourself an idol, or any likeness of what is in heaven above or on the earth beneath or in the water under the earth. You shall not worship them or serve them; for I, the Lord your God, am a jealous God, visiting the iniquity of the fathers on the children, on the third and fourth generation on those who hate Me, but showing loving kindness to thousands, to those who love Me and keep My commandments."

The problem with the standard cosmology is that it is a form of nature worship. Humanists believe, as stated in the Humanist Manifesto - their version of the Ten Commandments - that the universe is self-created; that there is no need for a creator. The humanist universe is therefore an alternate god. The implication for believers in God is that we must resist bringing these humanistic ideas into our theology about the creation. God makes it clear in Exodus 20 that He won't tolerate it, and we would be irrational to violate His commandment.

While I was formulating this book, I had another revelation that I haven't heard expressed quite this way before. It is that God created the Earth before the stars. All humanist cosmologies have the primary content of the universe developing billions of years before the Earth. These cosmologies all share a process bias. They assume that the universe formed through a natural process which implies that our Earth had to be formed after the stars and our own Sun. It makes sense in terms of a process-oriented origin, but the order isn't required if the components of the universe were designed and constructed. Both creationist cosmologies incorporate the idea that the Earth came first.

We've searched Scripture to see what God says about the cosmos using keywords like stars, heavens, mazzaroth, and firmament. There is a lot more than just the familiar passages of Genesis and Exodus 20. Here is a summary of what Scripture reveals.

1. The cosmos is described as young. Genesis describes the creation as a six day event, but were the days 24-hours in length or were they just periods of time? We have previously considered Exodus 20:8-11 which reads, "Remember the sabbath day to hallow it. Six days shalt thou labour, and do all thy work; but the seventh day is the sabbath of Jehovah thy God: thou shalt not do any work, thou, nor thy son, nor thy daughter, thy bondman, nor thy handmaid, nor thy cattle, nor thy stranger that is within thy gates. For in six days Jehovah made the heavens and the earth, the sea, and all that is in them, and rested on the seventh day; therefore Jehovah blessed the sabbath day, and hallowed it." God describes His creation week as a model for man's work week. It hardly makes sense if

God's days were long periods of time. God comes back to this thought in Exodus 31:16-17 saying that the Sabbath is a perpetual sign between Him and the sons of Israel in remembrance of God's rest after a week of creation. He seems to be wrapping up the six day creation with commandments for people to continually recognize and remember it. It is stated so strongly that believers in God should take it to heart. The universe is young.

2. The universe (which embodies all of God's creation) was made through knowledge and wisdom, so it should be understandable as man gains knowledge. Proverbs 3:13-18 admonishes us to treasure the acquisition of knowledge. "Blessed is the man that findeth wisdom, and the man that getteth understanding. For the gain thereof is better than the gain of silver, and her revenue than fine gold. She is more precious than rubies; and all the things thou canst desire are not equal unto her. Length of days is in her right hand; in her left hand riches and honour. Her ways are ways of pleasantness, and all her paths are peace. She is a tree of life to them that lay hold upon her; and happy is he that retaineth her." The writer continues in 19-20 to point out that it is through the same kind of wisdom and knowledge that the Creator operated. "Jehovah by wisdom founded the earth; by understanding He established the heavens. By His knowledge the deeps were broken up, and the skies drop down the dew." Western science and technology was founded by Christians who trusted God's Word that His creation could be studied because it was created by a reasonable God whose creation should be comprehensible. Psalm 8:3 calls the moon and stars the work of God's fingers. He spoke matter into existence, but He fashioned that matter into the stars and heavens. Proverbs 8:22-35 describes how the Creator existed before any of the creation.

3. We think of space as the absence of matter, but the heavens seem to have substance. Dozens of verses refer to space being spread out or stretched including Job 9:8, Psalm 104:2, Isaiah 40:22, Zechariah 12:1. Isaiah 50:3 even refers to the heavens as being clothed in black and sackcloth. Yes, it could just be poetic language, but you can only stretch or cloth something that has substance. The stretching of the heavens implies that secular

scientists are on the right track when they theorize that space has been stretched out. The Big Bang model is not an explosion, but what cosmologists refer to as inflation. This is not to say that Big Bang cosmology is Biblical or true, but that it is based on the right observation. The predictions of the Bible have preceded what humanistic scientists have finally recognized.

4. God is sustaining the universe with His invisible power. "He (Christ) is the image of the invisible God, the first-born of all creation; for in him all things were created, in heaven and on earth, visible and invisible... all things were created through him and for him. He is before all things, and in him all things hold together" (Col 1:15-17). The Bible predicts that invisible power maintains the universe, a concept which scientists have finally embraced through their ideas about dark matter and energy.

What the Bible says about the universe can be summarized as follows. It is young. It has an information basis. The fabric of space has substance and has been stretched out. The universe is being sustained by a power we can't see. The order of its creation is defined by Genesis as light and space first, then the Earth, and finally the stars and sun and moon to support the Earth. Interesting.

Creationist Cosmology

Although several scientists have suggested creationist explanations for the origin and nature of the universe, we're going to feature two ideas. We have a strategy in doing this based on the reality that we can't truly know how the universe came about in detail. One of the theories we're offering is based on the same concepts as the Big Bang, so it has the advantage of sharing all the accepted evidences for the standard cosmology. It demonstrates how Big Bang cosmologies have no inherent requirement for Earth being billions of years old or for starlight being ancient according to Earth-time. However, I suspect that Einsteinian physics and the cosmologies derived from it are flawed. Einstein himself was dissatisfied with his own solutions. For that reason, our second creationist cosmology will attempt to explain the thinking behind a departure from current ideas of physics and the nature of the universe.

The White Hole

Dr. Russ Humphreys has developed a suggestion which has been called White Hole Cosmology, a variation of standard Big Bang theory. Humphreys' theory shares the popular credibility of the Big Bang and associated Einstein relativity concepts. The strength of the theory is that it shares so much with the mainstream ideas that have been subject to great scientific scrutiny.

Dr. Humphreys took the Scriptural references related earlier and applied his knowledge of physics and general relativity to produce an alternative to the standard Big Bang. Humphreys' primary intent was to reconcile the light from distant stars with a young Earth. He assumes that the redshift of distant stars is the result of an expanding universe just as humanistic scientists believe. Humphreys' model begins with a white hole containing all the matter in the universe as God spoke it into existence. A white hole is the unstable opposite of a black hole. Where a black hole gravitationally absorbs matter and energy, white holes emit them and empty themselves over time. Since any white hole that ever existed emptied itself rapidly, we shouldn't expect to observe white holes any longer. According to general relativity, time and speed and gravity are related. Humphrey's theory says that God created Earth at the center of the white hole where it remained stationary while the rest of the matter and energy was stretched outward from the white hole at high velocities. Billions of years could therefore take place at the periphery of the white hole expansion while only thousands of years take place on Earth nearest the initial concentration of mass. Starlight would have billions of years of travel time while only a short time occurred on Earth.

The Humphreys cosmology demonstrates how the predictions of the Bible, the observations of scientists, and the application of modern physics theory can be combined to produce a viable explanation of how God created the universe while also accounting for the apparent billions of years of age in the cosmos. As mentioned earlier, the strength of Humphreys' idea is that it is only a subtle variant of the standard cosmology which therefore has all the same scientific credibility. The Humphreys cosmology establishes humanist and theist cosmologies on equal footing.

With that said, I personally find relativistic time dilation concepts unreasonable. At the time of Humphreys' White Hole cosmology or the Big Bang cosmology, the entire universe was created at once. What does it really mean when we suggest some objects are billions of years old and some are thousands of years old based on time dilation theories? We intuitively believe that now is now. Now isn't billions of years ago just because it's in some other place. It may just be possible that both the Big Bang and the White Hole are built upon established, but erroneous, ideas in physics. That's my segue to a radical departure from relativistic ideas in physics.

The Star Trek Universe

The second theistic idea about the universe that we are offering I like to call the Star Trek Cosmology, because it not only conforms with a Biblical understanding of the universe, but it allows us to travel to the stars. You see, if relativistic theories about physics and the universe are true and the speed of light is an absolute limit, travel beyond our solar system is impossible. Consider that the nearest star from our system is Proxima Centauri at a bit over 4 light years distant. Then consider that, according to relativity, a spacecraft's mass increases toward infinity as it accelerates toward the speed of light. Long before it reaches light speed, a spacecraft's increasing mass will prevent its propulsion unit from accelerating it faster. At a quarter the speed of light, a round trip to the nearest star is close to 40 years, and the spacecraft's inhabitants would waste their adult lifetimes to make the trip. It might be doable, but hardly a thrilling Star Trek adventure. When you consider that most stars are considerably farther away than Proxima Centauri, our desire for adventure in the next frontier is hopeless.

That's just one of the reasons I truly hope that Einstein was wrong. There is an alternative to relativity that depends on our understanding of matter at the atomic level. To understand it, we must consider the ideas of physicists before the age of Einstein, relativity, and all the strange modern variants of physics concocted to explain the disobedient behaviors of matter and energy.

James Clerk Maxwell was an earlier pioneer in physics whose equations are famous in the world of electrodynamics, and physics and engineering students the world over wear T-shirts sporting them. For our purposes, it is not important to list them or explain their workings. For purposes of cosmology, we're more interested in the implications of Maxwell's equations. Maxwell's work showed that light was electromagnetic in origin. Maxwell proposed that matter and light were electromagnetic phenomena affected by the magnetic fields emanating from positive and negative charges in the atom. Maxwell's derivation states that, completely contrary to Einstein's theory, light is exclusively an electromagnetic wave, and the speed of light is a variable, even in the vacuum of deep space. It is slower near celestial systems and faster away from the mass of celestial bodies. As the electric and magnetic fields and constants from electric charges in the atoms of these bodies of matter decrease in deep space, then the speed of light will increase exponentially. The speed of light varies with electric and magnetic field strengths and is not constant as Einstein affirms.

Modern day adherents to Maxwell's ideas assert that light slows in proximity to magnetic fields in proximity to mass and increases in velocity in deep space where magnetic fields are weak. Light from even the most distant objects could get to Earth in hours, days, or weeks if it travels most of the distance through deep space at velocities approaching infinity. As far as space travel is concerned, we can accept the speed of light as a limit if that speed is nearly infinite in deep space. It would mean that the Star Trek Enterprise could travel multiple times the Earth-reference speed of light once the Enterprise gets away from our solar system. Search the internet for "Pioneer Anomaly" and the "Shapiro Delay Effect" (which suggests that light slows nearer the electromagnetic center of our solar system) if you want to read about potential real-world examples of changing light speed. Note that the concept of a light year in Maxwell's universe is nonsensical, and so are the billions of years implied by light years. Light from the most distance reaches of the universe reached Earth in days, not billions of years.

Recently, a group of researchers have been promoting the concept of the Electric Universe asserting that gravity is too weak a force to account for the structures we observe in space. Similar to Maxwell, they claim that electricity and electromagnetism are the strong forces that shape such structures as galaxies and nebulae. They even suggest that the power of the Sun is primarily derived from the electromagnetic fields permeating space. For more information, search the web for the Thunderbolt Project.

Beyond Relativity

Many creationists are calling for a physics and cosmology revolution. So let's take a quick aside to talk about time being variable. If general relativity is not true, then all of the other derivations from general relativity such as time dilation, warped space, dimension contraction, time worm holes, black holes, etc. are invalid also. Proponents of the electromagnetic theory of Maxwell, Ives, Essen, Barnes, Lucas, Bergmann, and others offer a much better science for a young earth/young universe creation model than the young earth/old universe using Einstein relativity and the time dilation.

It's a radical idea in one sense, but also a conservative idea rooted in classical physics. Because the modern physics establishment is dominated by humanistic thought, it may be some time before another great physics mind comes along to champion this creationist alternative to Einstein's relativity. Meanwhile, Captain Kirk is waiting for his opportunity to seek new worlds and new civilizations.

The takeaway from our two creationist cosmologies is this. There is nothing in modern cosmology to undermine a straightforward reading of Genesis. Although the age of the universe is considered a side issue by some, Big Bang cosmology and alternate ideas about physics are both consistent with a Biblical timeframe of just thousands of years. We therefore are encouraged to continue presenting the Biblical timeframe as a viable model of science.

Other Signs Of Design

Isn't the universe just too big for somebody to have built it? That's our intuitive reaction, but then we also see the clockwork regularity of it. But regularity and precision isn't enough to convince us. Genesis says that celestial bodies were placed as signs. Below are two very diverse examples of the evidence of design in this huge cosmos of ours.

The Privileged Planet

Intelligent design researchers at the Discovery Institute have been pioneers in identifying evidence of design in nature. In their Privileged Planet book and companion video they uncover layers of circumstances that make Earth's surface features and materials just right to be inhabited, that place it in a solar system that provides just the right warmth and protection from comic collision, that place the solar system in just the right portion of the galaxy where other stars are neither too plentiful nor too sparse. All of these factors make our planet just right for intelligent life to develop and thrive. Then they make the connection that the same factors which make our planet habitable also make it right for us to examine and understand our universe. For example, if our solar system was located nearer the center of the galaxy, the intensity of starlight would interfere with our observation of the night sky. Of course, if God created everything as both a friendly environment and a learning laboratory for mankind, then all these factors make sense.

Evolutionary scientists dismiss the notion that Earth was designed for life by flipping the argument to say we evolved in a way that makes us suitable for the planet. However, it's curious that evolved monkeys like us are such capable explorers and that even the vastness of space is available to us. Where is the evolutionary advantage of that?

The universe seems to be full of signs that tell us about benevolent design. The people at the Discovery Institute search out these kinds of fortunate "coincidences" in the natural world that are best explained as designed structures and intentional circumstances. Check them out at www.discovery.org.

The Gospel In The Stars

But couched in mystery and ancient science are the stories told in the stars and formations of stars we call constellations. Genesis says that the stars were placed in the heavens for signs and for seasons. We all recognize the seasonal changes marked by the apparent movement of constellations, but what of the constellations themselves? The original meaning of the constellations is lost in antiquity. Their names and stories have been around as far back as we can look in human history. During the course of time, those stories have been distorted and co-opted by more recent cultures, like the Greeks, to conform to and support their legends, but the oldest meanings from early Biblical history support the idea of a story given by God.

Most of the modern interest in the Gospel revealed through the constellations comes from a handful of researchers who delved into documents a millennia old. A woman named Francis Rolleston is credited with compiling much of the research in her book, Mazzaroth: or, The Constellations. Her sources included the Arab astronomer Albumazer from about 850 A.D. and Tartar prince Ulugh Beigh from the time of Columbus, but these men were merely passing along information predating them by many centuries. Then contemporaries of Rolleston, Dr. Joseph Seiss and E. W. Bullinger, further developed and refined the work over a century ago. However, the late D. James Kennedy did us all the great favor of transforming the rather dry and scholarly 19th century literary style into a modern popular format in The Real Meaning Of The Zodiac. The following is merely an overview.

Just look at the constellations! There, right in front of us, is the Virgin, the Mother and Child, the serpent, the King, a Crown, the serpent going after the crown, the Great Physician grasping the serpent, the serpent striking a man's heel, the dying sacrifice, and the living fish which is the symbol of the Church. There is an altar, an arrow, a cross, a stream of water symbolizing the Holy Spirit being poured out into the fish's mouth, and of course the Lion triumphantly returning. Jesus was called "The Lion of Judah."

Perhaps on the Fourth Day of Creation, the Gospel message was written by the hand of God in the heavens long before He inspired men to write His Gospel on paper. The precious Gospel therefore is given to us by the book of God's nature as well as the book of God's Word. The original salvation plan of God for His people was given to Adam in the Garden of Eden with the heavens as a kind of visual aid to assist Adam in remembering and passing it on to future generations. Imagine God walking with Adam in the evenings, pointing out the constellations, and explaining everything to him.

God said that the lights in the sky were to be for signs, and a sign is something that proclaims a message. Christians have largely turned away from the study of the stars and the Zodiac because of the false teachings of astrology. The word Zodiac comes from the root `zoad' which comes from the ancient Hebrew word `sodi' which means a way, a path or a step. Thus the zodiac pictures show the path or the Way of Salvation. These same twelve major constellations are found in ancient Rome, Egypt, Persia, Babylon, and China. The constellations stand for the same things even though the groupings of stars don't really look like the things they represent. This at the very least means that probably there was originally one source for the designations of the constellations.

The Book of Job, the oldest book in the Bible written over 4000 years ago, speaks of the constellations. "Can you bind the beautiful Pleiades? Can you loose the cords of Orion? Can you bring forth the constellations in their seasons or lead out the Great Bear with its cubs? Do you know the laws of heaven? " (Job 38:31-33) God would not be pointing out the constellations if they were evil. God intended the stars as signs and remembrances of His plan for mankind.

Arabic tradition says that Seth and Enoch were the original founders of the ancient understanding of the stars and their signs and the meanings of their ancient names (Seiss 1972). The twelve major signs seem to move around the ecliptic, or the path the sun travels through the heavens as the Earth rotates. They are the twelve houses or tabernacles of the sun. Each one of them has associated with it three decans. The word decan comes from the word meaning `piece'. These minor constellations each tell a piece of the story and help to further explain the meaning of the major signs. Each major constellation takes up thirty degrees of the sky; with twelve times thirty equaling the 360 degrees of a complete circle. It is interesting to note that there are twelve chapters in the heavenly story, twelve months in a year, twelve tribes of Israel, and twelve Apostles. The number "12" signifies governing completion.

The following descriptions of the constellations and the stars are derived from The Gospel In The Stars written by Joseph A. Seiss in 1882.

1. **Virgo, The Virgin** - The zodiac begins with Virgo and ends with Leo. We start with the Virgin Mary and end with Jesus, the Lion of Judah. All traditional names and mythological names emphasize the virginity of the person represented in Virgo. She is pictured holding a sheaf of wheat, the spica, the best of the seed, which is indicated by the brightest star in this constellation, Al Zimach or Spica. Genesis refers to the Seed of Woman as an obvious reference to Christ. It seems appropriate that seed of wheat is depicted and that Christ became known as The Bread of Life. In the other hand she holds a branch. The ancient names of the stars in this constellation emphasize the importance of the Branch. Al Zimach

means the shoot, Al Azal means the branch, and Subilon means the ear of wheat.

    a. Coma - This constellation, the first decan of Virgo, denotes a pure virgin sitting on a throne feeding an infant boy who has a Hebrew name. The Hebrew word Coma, means the desired one, or the longed-for, and is the same word used to describe Christ as "the Desire of all nations."

    b. Centaurus - The centaurs of legend were two creatures in one, just as Christ is both God and man having two natures in one being. The legend of the centaur, Cheiron, says that even though he was immortal, he willingly died so that his friend could live. The name of this constellation in Hebrew means the despised. The brightest star is called Cheiron, which is the Hebrew root for 'the pierced'. Biblical prophesies about Christ say that he was pierced for our transgressions and despised in appearance.

    c. Bootes, The Coming One - The third decan is the figure of a strong man with a staff in his hand. This is a picture of the Good Shepherd looking over his flock. The Greeks confused this man with a ploughman, but the name of the brightest star in Bootes is Arcturus which is the watcher or the keeper, and Arktos is the enclosure or the fold. The star on the right side of Bootes is Al Katurops, which means the Branch or the Rod and is connected with the shepherd's staff.

2. **Libra, The Scales** - The balance scales stands for justice and equity. Scripture says that Christ paid the required price for our sin according to the system of justice from the Father. The name of this constellation in Hebrew is Mozanaim, and means the scales, weighing. In Arabic it is Al Zubena, which is the purchase, or redemption, or gain. In Coptic, Lambadia means house of propitiation and in Arabic, Lam is graciousness and badia is the branch - again showing the atoning grace of the Branch. The name of a star in one side of the scales of Libra is Zuben al Genubi, the price deficient. A star on the other side of the scales is Zuben al Shemali, the price which covers. Other names are Al Gubi, heaped up high, and Zuben Akrabi, the price of the conflict. One star is

simply called Tau, the last letter in the Hebrew alphabet, which is written as a cross and signifies the end, the completion.
   a. Crux, the Southern Cross - This constellation is distinctly defined by four stars in the form of a cross. It is no longer visible from the northern latitudes because of the gradual precession or wobble of the Earth's axis and was last seen in the horizons of Jerusalem at the time of Christ. The Hebrew name, Adom, means cutting off, just as Christ was cut off from His Father as He took upon Himself all the sins of the world for all time. Seiss wrote, "It was placed there as the sign of what holy prophecy had declared should come. It is the Cross of Calvary prefigured on the sky in token of the price at which our redemption was to be bought."
   b. Victima, The Slain Victim - Christ was slain for our sins and is seen represented here as the slain victim being pierced by the Centaurus who represents Christ, so we have the picture of Christ sacrificing Himself.
   c. Corona, the Crown - The third decan of Libra is the Corona Borealis, the Northern Crown, and it is vertically over Jerusalem once a month. This symbolizes the Lord Jesus, who willingly sacrificed Himself for us and is crowned King of Kings.
3. **Scorpio, The Scorpion** - The Arabic name is Al Akrab, which means scorpion and also wounding, conflict and war. The name in Coptic is Isidis, and means attack of the enemy. The main star located in the middle of the constellation is Antares which means wounding, cutting, tearing. The tail of the scorpion is raised ready to strike.
   a. Serpens, the Serpent - The serpent is seen going for the Crown, but being held and conquered by Ophiuchus. Satan took the form of a serpent in the Garden of Eden and is called the Dragon, the old serpent and the Devil.
   b. Ophiuchus - This constellation is depicted as the figure of a strong man wrestling with and defeating the serpent so that he does not get the crown. One foot of the man, by the scorpion's tail, is lifted up as if struck and the other foot is stomping on the head of the scorpion. This man is described as the Healer, the Physician, the Desired One.

c. Hercules - We see the figure of another very strong man. He is down on his right knee with his foot lifted up as though it was wounded, another type of Jesus. With his left foot, he is stepping on the head of Draco, the great dragon. He is holding a three-headed serpent in one hand and a club in the other. The Egyptian name for this sign means Him who comes. The brightest star in the constellation is in the head of the man and is called Rash al Ghetto which means the head of him who bruises. The name of the second star means the Branch kneeling. The Phoenicians worshipped a man called Hercules long before the Greeks heard of him. The Greeks liked the stories of the strength and power of this man, so they incorporated him into their mythology. In Genesis, God curses the serpent saying, "I will put enmity between you and the woman, and between your seed and her seed; he shall bruise your head, and you shall bruise his heel."

4. **Sagittarius, The Archer** - In this sign we see the centaur again, who in all languages is known in this constellation as the Archer, the Bowman, or He who sends forth the arrow. He is aiming his arrow at the scorpion, just as Christ overcame Satan.

    a. Lyra, The Harp - This constellation contains one of the brightest stars in the northern hemisphere, Vega. This figure of the harp, the oldest of the stringed instruments, denotes gladness, joy, and praise, praising the Archer for his achievements. Vega is the word from which we get our root word for victory.

    b. Ara, The Altar - The Greek word, Ara, means a small elevation of wood or stone used as an altar for sacrifices or a funeral pile. The Arabs call it Al Mugamra, meaning the completing, the finishing.

    c. Draco, The Dragon - The dragon, is a Biblical symbol for Satan. The star names in this constellation describe the dragon. Al Waid means one who is to be destroyed, Thuban means the subtle or crafty, and Al Dib means the reptile. The bright star Rastsban means the head of the Serpent. Other stars are Grumian - the deceiver, El Athik - the fraudulent, El Asiek - the one brought down, Gianser - the punished enemy, and Ethanin - the long serpent. Thuban, in the second coil of the serpent's tail, used to be the Pole Star about 4700 years ago. That made Satan the symbolic ruler of that age. The pole star is now Polaris in the tail of Ursa Minor, which means not only the bear but also " the fold", which would be the Church. Satan lost his prominence, and the honor of having the pole star went to the Church.

5. **Capricornus, The Goat** - The figure of Capricornus has the front half of a goat that is fallen or dying, and the back half is a fish tail that is alive and wiggling. The goat is a sacrificial animal used by Moses in the desert as a sin offering. The names of the stars in this sign all point to this sacrifice, such as Ma'Asad, the slaying, which gives the picture of the atoning sacrifice.

   a. Sagitta, The Arrow - There is no bow associated with this arrow: it is in flight, sent from an unseen hand to do the work of the piercing and slaying of Christ.

   b. Aquila - Aquila is the pierced, wounded and falling eagle. It is another symbol of Christ dying for the Church. The brightest star in this constellation is Al Tair which means the wounded. The second star is Tarared which means the scarlet-colored or covered with blood. The names of other stars mean the torn and the wounded in the heel. Joseph Seiss describes the eagle in this way: "The eagle is a royal bird, and the natural enemy of the serpent. It is elevated in its habits, strong and swift. It is very careful and tender toward its young, and is said to tear itself to nourish them with its own blood when all other means fail. And here is the noble Eagle, the promised Seed of the woman, pierced, torn and bleeding, that those begotten in His image may be saved from death, sheltered, protected and made to live for ever."

   c. Delphinus, The Dolphin - The third decan of Capricornus is the figure of a lively fish jumping up, the symbol of the fish which was used by the early Church.

6. **Aquarius, The Water-Bearer** - This constellation speaks of the joy of God's Spirit poured out on His people as the fruit of Jesus' victory. There is the figure of a man pouring water out of an urn that turns into a rushing stream. At the end of that stream is a fish, the Church, drinking in this blessing, as Jesus said He would do: "I will pour out my Spirit

on all flesh". (Isaiah 44:3) The Greeks called him Ganymede, the bright, glorified, and happy one. The main star on the man's right shoulder is Sa'ad al Melik, which means the Record of the out-pouring. The Greek and Latin names of this sign mean the pourer forth of water, the exalted Waterman.

- a. Pisces Australis, The Southern Fish - Here is seen the fish, the symbol of the Church, drinking in the stream. Jesus said, "If a man is thirsty, let him come to me and drink" (Rev. 12:6), and we see that happening right here with the fish drinking in and being immersed in the heavenly waters of the Holy Spirit that are being poured out.
- b. Pegasus, The Winged Horse - The Greeks called this the horse of the gushing fountain. Pega means the chief; and sus means horse and swiftly coming. The names of the stars are Markab, the returning; Scheat, he who goes and returns; Enif, the Branch; Al Genib, who carries; Homan, the waters; Matar, who causes the plentiful overflow. All the names of these stars fit very nicely with the picture of Aquarius.
- c. Cygnus, The Swan - The swan is a beautiful bird held sacred by some civilizations. The bird is in flight with its wings outspread to form a beautiful cross. The brightest star is Deneb, which means the Lord or Judge to come. Azel means one who goes and returns. Fafage means glorious, shining forth. Sadr means one who returns as in a circle. These names symbolize the returning of the Lord.

7. **Pisces, The Fishes** - This constellation contains two fish which are headed in different directions. The two fish are bound together by a long cord that is being held by the foot of the Ram in the next constellation. The Hebrew, Arabic, Greek and Latin names for this sign all mean the Fishes. In Coptic, its name is Pi-cot Orion, meaning the Fish, congregation, or the company of the coming Prince. The two fish represent a multitude of people that would be the Church. One fish represents Moses and the Old Testament prophets who foretold the coming of the Savior, and the other fish represents the New Testament Church that came into being after Jesus came to earth.

a. The Band, the Bridle - The ancient name of this sign is Al Risha, which means the band or the bridle, or unity. Tying the two fish together shows us that the Old Testament Church of the Patriarchs is tied to the Christian Church. The Band that unites these two Fishes is being held by the next sign, Aries the Ram or Lamb. This beautiful picture shows us that both parts of the Church belong to Christ, the Lamb of God.

b. Cephus, The Crowned King - The next decan gives us the picture of the exalted Jesus, enthroned on high, wearing a royal robe, a crown of stars, and holding a branch in His hand. In His right shoulder is the bright star, Al Deramin, which means, the Quickly-returning. Other stars are Al Phirk - the Redeemer and Al Rai - the Shepherd. The name Cephus means the Royal Branch or the King.

c. Andromeda, The Chained Queen - This is another picture of the Church as the Bride of Christ. But this woman is in chains, tied down by her wrists and ankles. This is the picture of the Church here on earth, tied down by the confines of this earthly existence.

8. **Aries, The Ram** - This sign is the Ram or the Lamb signifying the Lamb of God.

   a. Cassiopeia, The Enthroned Queen - This is the figure of a woman now sitting on a throne, a picture of God's Church lifted out of evil, no longer restrained by earthly bonds. She is enthroned on high with the Great King. The name Cassiopeia, means the beautiful or the enthroned. To the right of the Queen is Cephus, the Crowned King, holding his sceptre toward her as though to proclaim her his Bride.

   b. Cetus, The Sea Monster - This figure is the Leviathan of the Book of Job. A star of this sign is called Mira which means the Rebel and is a variable star that shines brightly, then gradually becomes invisible about every three hundred days. This symbolizes Satan who is the Deceiver. The names of the stars in Cetus are Menkar, which means the chained enemy; and Diphda, the Overthrown or Thrust-down.

   c. Perseus, The Breaker - Pictured is a man who breaks the Deceiver and carries a sword and the head of Medusa. The names of stars in Perseus are Atik, He who breaks; Al Genib, the One who carried away; and Mirfak, who helps. The head he carries under his arm is that of Medusa, which means 'the Trodden under foot'. The name of the brightest star in the head is Al Ghoul or Algol, which means the Evil Spirit. Names of other stars in the head are Rosh Satan, Satan's head; Al Oneh, the Weakened, the Subdued. In these symbols we have the picture of the Lamb of God who breaks the power of the Evil One and raises His Bride to the status of the Enthroned Queen.

9. **Taurus, The Bull** - This figure of a rampaging bull signifies the glorious coming of our Lord Jesus Christ. It is interesting to note that this rampaging bull is rising up out of Aries, the Lamb of God. Riding on the shoulders of the bull is a grouping of seven stars called the Pleiades, representing the Church as in the Book of Revelation.

   a. Orion, The Huntsman or The Glorious One - Here in this sign is a mighty hunter holding a lion skin in one hand and a club raised in the other. He is most easily identified by the band of three stars that make up his belt. From his belt hangs a sword with a lamb's head for the handle, and his foot is stomping on the head of Lepus, the enemy. The name of this very prominent and beautiful constellation is Orion, which means He who comes forth as light, the Brilliant, the Swift. In his right shoulder is a bright star called Betelguese, which means the Branch coming. On the other shoulder is Bellatrix, which means Swiftly coming or Suddenly destroying. In his foot that is stomping and crushing the Lepus is Rigel, which means the Foot that Crushes. The three bright stars in his belt are Mintaka, Al Nitam, Al Nitah, and are called, "the Three Kings", or "Jacob's Rod".

   b. Eridanus, The River of the Judge or the Fiery Stream - From under the raised foot of Orion comes the Fiery Stream of the River of the Judge. Many times in the Bible we find reference to the River of the Judge or the Fiery Stream that issues forth judgment, and it is seen here flowing between Taurus and Orion.

   c. Auriga, The Shepherd - In this third decan of Taurus, seated with the Rampaging Bull, the Mighty Huntsman, and the fiery River of Judgment, is pictured the Good Shepherd. This man is sitting on the Milky Way and is holding a mother goat and her kids in his left arm.

Auriga in Latin means a conductor of the reins or coachman. This man holds a band in his other hand that is the same band used to guide the Fishes and to bind the enemy. The brightest star in this constellation is Capella which lies at the heart of the mother goat. The forelegs of the goat are wrapped around the neck of the Shepherd. This is a beautiful picture of the Good Shepherd caring for His flock.

10. **Gemini, The Twins** - Rather than two children being born at the same time, this sign of two people sitting together represents the union of Christ with His Bride. The first figure holds a club in his hand with his other arm around the second figure. The second figure is holding a harp in one hand and a bow and arrow in the other. The word Gemini in the original Hebrew does not mean two children born at the same time, but rather signifies the completion of a betrothal. The Coptic name Pi Mahi means the United, the Completely joined. In the foot of the first figure is the star All Henah, the Hurt, the Wounded. The Bright star in his head is called Polluz, which means the Judge, and is sometimes called Hercules, the Mighty Sufferer. In his waist is the star Wasat which means Set, Seated or Put in Place. The Egyptians called this figure Hor or Horus, which means The Coming One, the son of light, the slayer of the serpent, the recoverer of the dominion. In the head of the second figure is the star called Castor or Apollo, which means the Coming Ruler or Judge, born of the light. This sign then represents the marriage of the Lamb and the union of Christ with his Bride. Jesus is the Son of God; and since we who are the Church are called joint heirs with Christ and brothers of Jesus, we are also sons of God and in this sense the Gemini symbol could also signify twins in the brotherly sense.

   a. Lepus, The Hare or The Enemy - This sign is the figure of a rabbit or hare. In Arabic the name Arnebeth means the Hare, but it can also mean the Enemy of the Coming. In Egyptian the name is Bashti-Beki and means the Offender confounded. The names of the stars in this sign are Nibal - the Mad, Rakis - the Caught, and Sugia - the Deceiver. Remember that Orion is stomping on his head.

   b. Canis Major, The Great Dog - Canis Major is the Great Dog who is the devourer of the Hare. The main star here is Sirius, which is usually the brightest star we can see. Sirius means Prince, Guardian, the Victorious. The name of this figure in Egyptian is Naz-Seir, which means the Sent Prince. Jesus was referred to as the Nazarene. Here is a picture of the Victorious Christ.

   c. Canis Minor, The Second Dog - In Egyptian it is called Sebak, which means conquering, victorious. The name of the brightest star in this sign is Procyon, which means Redeemed or Redeeming. The second brightest star is Al Gomeiza, which also refers to redemption and means burdened or enduring for the sake of others.

11.**Cancer, The Crab** - Whereas "cancer" conjures up negative images of disease, this cancer represents protection. The crab is known for its powerful claws that hold on tightly to whatever is in its grasp. As the crab grows, it must completely remove its old shell and grow a new one. When a person accepts the Lord as Savior, it is said that he puts off the old man or the old nature and puts on the new man who is clothed with righteousness. In the center of this constellation is a cluster of stars called the Praesepe or the Manger. In Hebrew and Arabic it means the Multitude, Offspring, the Young, the Innumerable Seed. In Latin Praesepe means the place where the animals are fed, or the stable. An interesting astronomical observation is that this sign of the Manger and the Northern Cross only appear in the sky together during the week around Christmas. As the constellation of Cygnus rises in the evening, it begins to travel across the lower part of the sky and turn upside down forming the Northern Cross. Then just before dawn during the Christmas Week, the Praesepe or Manger, rises above the horizon to be seen in the sky with the Cross. What amazing wonders and signs the Lord has given us! Egyptians call this constellation of the Crab, Klaria, the Folds, the Resting-places. We get the name Cancer from the Noetic word, Khancer. Khan means the traveler's resting-place, and cer means embraced or encircled; therefore, Cancer means rest secured. This sign then represents the eternal rest for the saints of God. It shows Christ's possessions held secure.

   a. Ursa Minor, The Lesser Bear - The two constellations of the Lesser and Greater Bears were misnamed by the Greeks. The Egyptians,

Persians, and the Indians all considered these two signs to be the flocks of God. The bright star in Ursa Major is Dubeh, taken to mean bear; but the Hebrew word Dober, which was the original name, actually means a fold or collection of domestic animals. This would be a very strange looking bear with a very long tail. Taking the ancient Hebrew name, these two signs would be the Lesser and Greater Folds or Sheepfolds, symbolizing God's people, the sheep of His pasture. There are seven major stars in this constellation symbolizing the seven churches in Revelation, and it has a total of twenty-four stars, which suggests the twenty-four elders of Revelation. The names of the stars are Kochab which means the Star, Al Pherkadain - the Calves. Al Gedi - the Kid or the Chosen of the flock. and Al Kaid - the Assembled. The Greeks also called this constellation Arcas or Arx, which means the stronghold of the saved.

b. Ursa Major, The Great Bear - The names of the stars in this constellation further emphasize that the name of the sign should be the Great Sheepfold rather than the Great Bear. Al Naish or Annaish means the ordered or assembled together as sheep in a fold. Mizar means guarded or enclosed place, Dubheh means herd or fold, Merach means the flock, Cab'd al Asad means multitude of the assembled, Et Acolo is the sheepfold, Al Kaiad is the assembled, El Kaphrah means the protected or redeemed, and Dubheh Lachar is the latter herd or flock. The seven main stars of this group are sometimes called Aish, which means a community or a congregation.

c. Argo, The Ship - This sign is associated with the story of Jason and the Argonauts, brave travelers returning home victorious. The brightest star in the constellation is Canopus, the name of the helmsman of the Argo, which means the possession of Him who comes. Here we have a portrait in the stars of the multitudes of saints returning to their heavenly home.

12. **Leo, The Lion** - The earthly lion is known as the king of beasts. Jesus is known in Scripture as the Lion of the Tribe of Judah. The lion is always thought to be physically strong and fierce. The Lamb of God will return as the Lion tearing his enemies to pieces. This sign of the Lion is leap-

ing forth as a consuming fire. In Jewish astronomy the twelfth sign was the sign of Judah, so Leo truly represents the Lion of the Tribe of Judah. Other names of this sign are Aryeh - He who rends, Al Sad - He who tears and lays waste, Pi-mentekeon - the Pourer-out of rage, and Leon, the vehemently coming, the leaping forth as a consuming fire. The main star is Regulus, which means the feet which crush. The second star is Denebola, which is the Judge, the Lord who comes with haste. The names of the stars describe the Lion of Judah as He is described in Scripture - no mere coincidence.

 a. Hydra, The Fleeing Serpent - The name Hydra means the Abhorred. The names of stars in this constellation mean that the evil serpent is finally taken out of the way.
 b. Crater, The Cup of Wrath - God said that His wrath would be poured out into the cup of His indignation. This constellation gives us the picture of this cup or bowl of wrath planted into the back of the Hydra, putting God's wrath squarely on the serpent.
 c. Corvus, The Raven - The raven symbolized the bird of punishment. This bird is seen holding the serpent with its claws and tearing it with its beak. Two stars in this raven are Al Chiba, which means the Curse inflicted, and Minchir al Gorab, which means the Raven tearing to pieces. All four of these constellations together provide a picture of Christ overcoming sin and vanquishing Satan.

What is the truth? We gain knowledge and we lose knowledge. Because our ancestors didn't hand down to us the ancient knowledge contained in the stars, we have doubts. We may never know about the gospel written in the stars in its original form, but the vivid symbolism of these starry signs is too comprehensive to be coincidental. The heavens continue to declare the glory of God even to the modern astronomer who continues to use these ancient names. The orderliness and precision of the universe alone speak of the handiwork of God. But when you also consider that the stars were placed in Heaven, not just thrown there haphazardly by some explosion, it gives you an idea of the immensity of God's love for us. It is amazing to me that astronomers can look at these stars every night and have no understanding of the importance of the names of the stars. They are oblivious to the obvious signs. As Christians we need to take back ground by preserving the true meanings and passing them on to our children. We should no longer avoid studying the stars because of the association with the wickedness of astrology. God created those stars and He designed them to speak and show knowledge of Him, and we need to get excited about the things that His creation can teach us.

CHAPTER 4

The Story of Life

We Call Them Creatures

The story of life, biology, is both the origin of evolutionary thinking and its weakest link. The concept of evolution runs contrary to our intuition and our ancestry. In an age of evolutionary thought, we are struck by how our common language bears the evidence of our ancestral beliefs. People might speak of death as "going to meet our maker" regardless of whether they personally believe in creation or an after-life. We previously mentioned how "universe" refers to God speaking it into existence. And we call living things "creatures", a word derived from our innermost confidence that they are created things. Not evidence for creation, but evidence of our deepest beliefs about life on earth.

In this chapter we will be relating what we know, what we think we know, what God has told us, and what creationists suggest as an alternative to the standard theory. Let me simply state a few ideas as a preview of where this chapter is headed. Evolutionists can't create life and don't know how it could have created itself. Living things are so well segregated into various distinct kinds that evolutionary transitions between kind isn't suggested by the evidence. Our knowledge of genetics mitigates against evolution. It is so much like a computer language that we intuitively see it as an information system designed by an incredible mind. The Bible makes it amply clear that God did not use an evolutionary process to design living things. He says He created each kind of animal and that each one reproduces after its kind. He even gives warnings against trying to cross bread animals, perhaps because the offspring of a cross-bread animal is usually infertile.

What Scientists Observe About Life

What scientists observe about living things is a big subject that we will attempt to distill down to the essentials. According to a textbook of basic biology, all living things have five characteristics:

- They are organized. Every living thing is made up of parts that work together to facilitate the function of the whole.
- They metabolize. All living things consume energy in order to continue the processes of life.
- They react to stimuli. Living things must be able to perceive enough about their environment to acquire nourishment and protect themselves from damage. You see this in the way plants grow toward sunlight to facilitate photosynthesis or earthworms retreat from sunlight in order to maintain their moisture.
- They reproduce. Living things have to be self-replicating because all things die and must reproduce offspring in order for life to continue. Why must life continue? That's a profound philosophical concept that observation alone doesn't address.
- They evolve.

Huh? What does it mean that life evolves? Here is where humanistic thought has entered the textbook. We don't observe that living things evolve if we mean changing into other varieties. What we actually observe is that living things are managed by a genetic code that allows for great variation in offspring. It's really a corollary to the previous point regarding reproduction. Because the environment is subject to change, it must be possible (from a design point of view) for at least some offspring to be able to survive in a changing environment. Therefore the information system that controls life, allows for significant variety in offspring. The above textbook definition of life is inadequate to describe enough regarding what we observe about life. The textbook has an evolutionary bias, so it avoids fully revealing the observations that are inconsistent with an evolutionary worldview. Shedding that bias, we can add more observations.

Life always comes from life. It is the law of biogenesis. A law of biology, a principle we never see violated, is that every living thing comes from another living thing. In other words, children have parents. We never see living things develop spontaneously from non-living chemicals. This is a problem for any humanist theory because a humanist must assume that the first life developed from non-living chemicals by an undirected process. Or as creationist Kent Hovind enjoyed saying, "Evolutionists think we evolved from a rock."

We already mentioned that all living things are directed by a built in information system which we call genetics. In our experience, information systems, such as computer applications, don't develop spontaneously. Information systems are the product of intelligence. The genetic code is hard to explain separate from design.

Living things can be categorized into discrete kinds. We refer to the resulting system of classification as taxonomy. Many systems of classification have been proposed but the common theme is that living things can be classified according to similarity. At the system's broadest level, "kingdom", most biologists would agree that the differences between organisms in different kingdoms, such as plants and animals, are so extreme that they are permanently separated by their genetic makeup. Some would make this same assertion at the next level, the "phylum". In the animal kingdom, for example, the thirteen phyla are sponges, coelenterates, flatworms, mollusks, annelids, arachnids, crustaceans, insects, fish, amphibians, reptiles, birds, and mammals. It seems pretty intuitive that a sponge does not have the genetic makeup to become a mammal, although humanistic evolutionists might question that assertion. The point of universal agreement however is that there is no smooth merging from one type of living thing to another. We observe distinctly separate kinds of living things.

Another thing we observe about living things is they are interrelated. Biologists refer to symbiotic relationships where the very existence of one kind of organism depends on another organism. A current good example is the relationship between honeybees and flowering plants. Recently in the United States there has been a decline in the honeybee population which has lead to a concern that pollination of flowering plants will suffer with a resulting impact on agriculture. Explanations of these kinds of relationships in the area of origins always suffer from the "chicken and egg" argument. If the two very different kinds of organisms depend on each other for survival, how could they evolve separately? How did one survive until the other came into existence?

Nevertheless, such relationships are common and not just at the detail level. At the kingdom level, plants and animals have a necessary relationship. Plants utilize carbon dioxide and free the oxygen molecules back into the atmosphere. Animals need oxygen and release carbon dioxide into the atmosphere for plants to use. If there were no plants, the atmosphere would become poisoned by excessive carbon dioxide levels. Survival of both plants and animals requires a balance between them.

Finally, we observe that all living things have complexity in their structure and function. There are no "simple" life forms. Even a single-celled organism contains genetic information that defines its organization and enables reproduction. It's not just a blob of protoplasm as nineteenth century scientists supposed. To give you an idea of the complexity of a single celled organism, I quote the following from Encarta. Just skim it. It's only intended as an example to show how unsimple life is.

> *Prokaryotic cells are relatively small, ranging in size from 0.0001 to 0.003 mm (0.000004 to 0.0001 in) in diameter. With the exception of a few species, prokaryotic cells are surrounded by a protective cell wall. The cell walls of archaebacteria and bacteria contain forms of peptidoglycan, a protein-sugar molecule not present in the cell walls of fungi, plants, and certain other eukaryotes. The archaebacteria cell wall has a more diverse chemical composition than the cell wall of bacteria.*
>
> *Just inside the cell wall of prokaryotes is the plasma membrane, a thin structure that is both flexible and strong. In both prokaryotes and eukaryotes, the plasma membrane is composed of two layers of phospholipid molecules interspersed with proteins, and regulates the traffic that flows in and out of the cell. The prokaryotic plasma membrane, however, carries out additional functions. It participates in replication of deoxyribonucleic acid (DNA) for cell division and synthesis of adenosine triphosphate (ATP), an energy molecule. In some prokaryotes, the plasma membrane is essential for photosynthesis, the process that uses light energy to convert carbon dioxide and water to glucose.*

> *In the interior of the prokaryotic cell is the cytoplasm, a watery fluid that is rich in dissolved salts, nutrients, enzymes, and other molecules. The great majority of the cell's biochemical reactions, which number in the thousands, take place within the cytoplasm. Prokaryotic cells typically have a single molecule of DNA in a closed loop floating free in a region of the cytoplasm called the nucleoid. Many species of prokaryotes also contain DNA in tiny ringlets known as plasmids in the cytoplasm.*
>
> *Ribosomes, tiny beadlike structures that manufacture proteins, are also located in the cytoplasm. Ribosomes contain ribonucleic acid (RNA), a type of genetic material. The structure of ribosomal RNA in archaebacteria is different than the RNA structure found in bacteria, and scientists often use this feature to determine whether an organism belongs to the archaebacteria group or the bacteria group.*
>
> *With the exception of the ribosomes, prokaryotes lack organelles (specialized structures such as the nucleus, chloroplasts, mitochondria, lysosomes, and Golgi apparatus), which are present in eukaryotes (see Cell). Some photosynthetic archaebacteria and bacteria have internal membranes, extensions of the plasma membrane known as chromatophores or thylakoids, which contain the pigments for photosynthesis.*
>
> *Some species of prokaryotes form endospores, thick-walled, dehydrated structures that can resist extreme dryness and very high temperatures for long periods of time. Anthrax, tetanus, and botulism are diseases caused by endospore-forming bacteria.*
>
> *Certain prokaryotes, such as the bacteria Salmonella, move independently by using flagella, long structures that rotate in a propeller-like fashion. Prokaryotic flagella consist of intertwined fibrils (small fibers) of the protein flagellin. A prokaryote may have a single flagellum, have a group of flagella at one or both poles of the cell, or be covered with flagella. Many species of prokaryotes also have pili (singular, pilus)-slender, hairlike extensions used for attachment to soil, rocks, teeth, or other structures.*

As you can see, there is considerable complexity in even the smallest organisms. Researchers are particularly intrigued by the flagellum which has been likened to a tiny outboard motor. Dr. Michael Behe has coined the term "irreducible complexity" to describe how the flagellum is made up of parts that must all be present before the flagellum is functional and provides survival advantages. He asks how all the parts could evolve based on natural selection when none of the parts on their own offer a selection advantage without all of them.

The Evolutionary Tale

Now that we have a summary of just some of the characteristics scientists observe, what then is the humanistic concept of biological history? According to the theory of evolution, life formed in the oceans perhaps four billion years ago from chemical reactions of molecules such as water, carbon dioxide, and methane. This origin of life was a one-time occurrence in the past that has never been observed in historical times. According to our present understanding, it happened in violation of the scientific law of biogenesis mentioned earlier. It was a miracle, a supernatural event. Oops. My creationist bias just slipped in there.

Nevertheless, if the humanistic understanding is correct, it must have happened. In the 1950's, Stanley Miller conducted an experiment to demonstrate how the first life could develop from chemicals. By carefully controlling the environment, Miller was able to create non-living organic chemicals. Nevertheless, his experiment was hailed as proof that life could develop spontaneously if the conditions on the early Earth were favorable. Let's get back to the humanist story.

The first life forms were one-celled organisms classified as prokaryotes because they lacked a cell nucleus. Although prokaryotes were the first life form, they exist today. Because these first living things developed from non-living chemicals, organic food didn't exist. Those first living things must have obtained energy from chemosynthesis, a chemical conversion of non-organic material to produce energy. Some time later cells evolved that could produce their own food by photosynthesis. Photosynthetic processes are responsible for enriching the oxygen content of the atmosphere, which enabled animal life to evolve, presumably from these photosynthesizing one-celled organisms.

According to the humanist story, single-celled organisms dominated for a couple of billion years, presumably gearing up for the next great revolution when multicellular life developed. At the time called the Cambrian period (about 500 million years ago) all of the major kinds of animals abruptly appear in the fossil record in what is called the Cambrian explosion. The leap from simple multi-celled organism to the development of skeletons, diversified organs, central nervous systems, sexual reproduction, and more is the source of endless speculation because the history and mechanisms for such change are unknown. Part of the power of the story in popular consciousness is that it is an endless source of storytelling. The so-called age of the dinosaurs is particularly compelling for children, providing a platform for humanists to influence young and impressionable minds with their story of life.

Homology, the similarity between living things, is an often-presented evidence for evolution, but homology is an interpretation, not an evidence. One can just as easily present a homology chart of motor vehicles showing the bicycle at the bottom and a Ferarri sports car at the top. The chart clearly demonstrates the similarity between wheeled vehicles, but the driving force is clearly design rather than undirected change over time. This and other arguments show us that humanistic evolution is an interpretive framework.

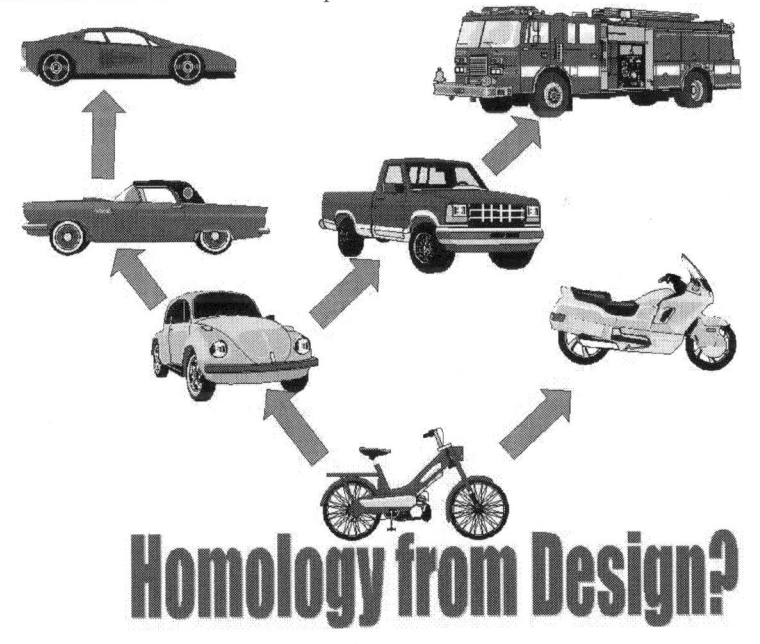

Homology from Design?

What Scripture Says

Let's begin our search for an alternative explanation by studying what the Bible tells us about the origin of life.

> *Gen 1:21 "And God created great whales, and every living creature that moveth, which the waters brought forth abundantly, after their kind, and every winged fowl after his kind: and God saw that it was good."*

We're told about a dozen times in Genesis that living things reproduce after their own kind. Although there may be controversy regarding what constitutes a "kind", it seems likely "kinds" are not the same as "species". Biologists recognize that dogs, wolves, and coyotes all developed from an original canine ancestor which is probably equivalent to the Biblical "kind". This means that the sheer number of animals which the Creator had to bioengineer is much less than the number of species. In the modern classification system, the "kind" is somewhere between Genus and Family.

> *Gen 1:26 "And God said, Let us make man in our image, after our likeness: and let them have dominion over the fish of the sea, and over the fowl of the air, and over the cattle, and over all the earth, and over every creeping thing that creepeth upon the earth."*

The Bible differentiates between Man and animals. Man is created in God's image and is positionally given dominion over the rest of life on Earth. Although Man has similarities to the animals in structure, we can't strictly apply what we learn about animals to Man.

> *Gen 1:29-30 reads that God said, "See I have given you every herb that yields seed which is on the face of the earth, and every tree whose fruit yields seed; to you shall it be for food. Also to every beast of the earth, to every bird of the air, and to every thing that creeps on the earth, in which there is life, I have given every green herb for food."*

God created a special relationship between plants and animals with plants essentially being food. This is really pretty profound if you think about it. We intuitively have no remorse when we consume a plant, but have second thoughts when it comes to killing an animal for food. Plants are food without guilt. Some creationists take these verses a step farther and assert that all animals were vegetarian in the beginning, but these verses don't say explicitly that animals only ate plants. It simply says that plants were given as a food source. An additional clue is given in Genesis 9:3 where God tells Noah that it's permissible for him to eat animals after the flood, which implies that Man was vegetarian up to that time.

Although we can lean toward the theory that men and animals were vegetarian, we can't be dogmatic about it. Some of my creationist friends will be upset because "no animal death" has become a creation doctrine even though it isn't generally a church doctrine. I sympathize with them, but my standard is to differentiate between my personal theories and what God says explicitly in the Bible. Did God create animals to be immortal? Were animals around long enough to get old and die before Adam sinned? Genesis doesn't say, and I don't want to dwell on ideas that may be a stumbling block to people.

> Gen 2:8-9 "And the LORD God planted a garden eastward in Eden; and there he put the man whom he had formed. And out of the ground made the LORD God to grow every tree that is pleasant to the sight, and good for food; the tree of life also in the midst of the garden, and the tree of knowledge of good and evil."

We shouldn't be misled by the garden of Eden and think that the early Earth was a paradise. A garden is a specially reserved plot of land cultivated to contain beneficial plants. This verse makes it clear that God created a special environment in the garden where favorable plants were cultivated. It was a protected retreat for Adam and Eve and not necessarily representative of the rest of the Earth. When you consider that Adam and Eve may have been in the garden for nearly a century based on Seth being born when Adam was 130 years old, there was a lot of time outside of the garden for living things to proliferate through the rest of the world. Scripture doesn't tell us about life outside of the garden.

> Gen: 9:1-3 explains that God blessed Noah and his sons, and said to them: "Be fruitful and multiply, and fill the earth. And the fear of you and dread of you shall be on every beast of the earth, on every bird of the air, on all that move on the earth, and on all the fish of the sea. They are given into your hand. Every moving thing that lives shall be food for you. I have given you all things, even as the green herbs."

We referenced earlier how man and animals may have been vegetarian, but circumstances changed after the Flood. This verse implies that man was vegetarian before the flood, and that god was releasing Noah and his family to eat animals. The practical reason for this change may have been that the flood had destroyed cultivated farmland, and animals were an immediate source of food.

Perhaps this is another reason why God gave Noah seven of every clean animal instead of just two.

These verses represent most of the clues that the Bible gives us regarding life on Earth. Bible teachers often make the claim that the initial creation was perfect, but this claim is based more on reverence for the Creator than it is on any explicit statements of Scripture. The Bible uses terms like "good" and "very good" to describe God's creation work, and certainly the presence of a lying serpent in the garden indicates that the creation was anything but perfect. But then again, what do we mean by "perfect"? If God's plan was to provide an environment to test Adam's loyalty, then the serpent was necessary. And if God wanted to create a special refuge in the Garden of Eden set apart from the rest of the world, then undesirable elements in the rest of creation were needed to contrast with the garden. The reason this point matters is that unbelievers sometimes point to faults in the natural world as evidence that it couldn't have been created by a perfect God. Such a claim is illogical. God had reasons to create an imperfect world, perfectly designed for His purposes. And after a while, Adam's sin and the resulting curse caused the creation to become even more corrupted from its "very good" beginning.

The Biblical View Of Life

"In the beginning God..." is the start of the creation story in Genesis, and God is a Creator with knowledge and power. In fact, we could say that God began His work with information and then devised a mechanism to store and interpret it. The Creator's software system is what we call genetics and His hardware is chemistry, DNA and proteins, and assorted other biochemical parts. From this amazing system of information and machinery, the Creator could engineer any type of living thing, and He seems to have worked from some sort of master plan to implement the complementary inter-relationship between living creatures to ensure their survival. Human scientists, regardless of their individual philosophy, have done an outstanding job in revealing God's information system.

Genesis says that God spoke the universe into existence, but what that means in detail we don't know. Chemistry is one of the foundational elements in the beginning. The creator arranged a few electrically significant particles – protons, electrons, and neutrons – into all the elements in what we call the Periodic Table...one of those miracles of design. One proton and it's hydrogen, two protons makes helium, and so on until you get all the unstable heavy elements. But the key bunch in the table for biological life is carbon, hydrogen, and oxygen. They represent the hardware of life from which all living things are manufactured. Those elements have unique characteristics allowing them to combine to form complex compounds which behave like microprocessors in the most sophisticated machines ever made.

Once the Creator decided on the hardware of life, He turned to the software side. The genetic code could be likened to an information system which utilizes hydrocarbons as its media. Similar to life's chemistry, the genetic code uses a building block approach to produce a broad array of living kinds with each kind having the ability to differentiate within kind to produce wonderful variety and increase the odds of survival. Does this sound a little bit like evolution? You bet! Creationists call this change within kind "microevolution". It's the scientific part of evolution theory. God created each kind of animal with genetic instructions that allow all kinds of superficial changes to help insure both survival and artistry. We'll learn later that after the flood of Noah's day, genetic variability allowed each kind to survive and diversify to repopulate the world in light of changes in the post-flood environment.

The Genesis account gives us a few insights regarding how the creation was assembled, notably starting with plants on the third day. Why plants? God was beginning with no organic material for animals to consume, so He began with organisms that could generate their own food from inorganic materials, a necessary first step in populating the biosphere. It's interesting that day three specifies that plants began on land, quite different from the evolutionary idea of life beginning in the oceans. The fossil record may be biased in this regard since the land has been subject to considerably more geological upheaval than the ocean floors resulting in fossils being obliterated as much as preserved. Much of the fossil record is made up of shelled sea life that is readily preserved when washed onto land, whereas plant life is more fragile. Therefore, even though sea creatures were created second on day five, they may appear to have come first in the fossil record. Undoubtedly, secular geologists may take issue with this, but it will be more based on their bias than on reason.

A prediction of the creation model is that the oldest fossil organisms that can be found will be land plants. Scientists are actually pretty close to reaching the same conclusion, currently believing the oldest fossils to be bacteria-like precursors to plants that could live without oxygen in inhospitable environments.

Genesis describes God working on one environment at a time, a process that makes intuitive sense to anyone who has been a builder. He began with land plants because they could create their own food. Equally important is the role of plant life in oxygenating the planet's atmosphere, a process on which animal life absolutely depends. Presumably the land plants colonized the oceans before the sea creatures are created on the fifth day so that the ocean water could be sufficiently oxygenated also. Genesis goes on to describe the creation of sea creatures and birds on the fifth day, and land animals and Man on the sixth day. Because the order of creation is so similar to what evolutionary scientists observe, it's little wonder that they could be misled by the evidence to come up with a wrong story. Secular scientists aren't taking advantage of the history left by the Creator.

You may be wondering what we mean by animal "kinds" and how they relate to modern taxonomy. The "kinds" describes in Genesis and referred to here lie somewhere between "family" and "genus" in the modern classification system. Kinds are very similar to the idea of "common names". For example, the common name "bear" relates to any animal in the family "Ursidae" which includes genera like the polar bear, black bear, grizzly, etc. There is a similar situation among the family "Canis" which includes dog and wolf varieties. Both creationist and evolutionary biologists recognize that all the dog-like animals may have had a common ancestor just like creationists know that all the varieties of men have a common ancestor in Adam through Noah's family. Thought of that way, "kinds" are pretty intuitive. Kinds include camels, cows, horses, bats, cats, etc.

I think you can see there is a lot of agreement between atheistic evolutionists and God-believing Biblical creationists because we are both looking at the same evidence. The basic difference is that creationists accept the observational reality without the add-on belief in one kind of animal morphing into another kind. The Biblical view of life is that life was created...engineered if you will. God created the "kinds" and coded each genome with enough genetic material to allow micro-evolution within each kind in order to ensure survival in a changing world. All of the kinds have been in existence from the beginning consistent with the fossil record Cambrian explosion evidence (although creationists tend to differ with the humanist time frame of millions of years). Consistent with the evidence, we expect to see living things easily classified according to kind. Because all living things were designed by the same Creator, we should expect to see similar body-part features among the kinds. The similarity is not from evolutionary development and common ancestry, but is rather the result of a good engineer using things that work for very different applications. Design similarities simply make sense.

The Fascinating Creatures Chronicles

If living things simply evolved from chance changes interacting favorably with environmental circumstances, living things and their behavior should be boring and functional. That's not how life is. Creatures exhibit fascinating, unexpected behaviors. They are surprisingly beautiful. They have skills that transcend competitive advantage. I've collected stories over the years, short vignettes about living things and their behaviors that point beyond mere adaptation. Wherever possible, I've given credit to authors or sources, but honestly I don't know where some of them came from since they can be as much as three decades old.

The Grunion - by Mark Stewart

On certain nights during the spring and summer, sandy California beaches are the scene of a spectacular display put on by small silvery fish called grunion. By the thousands, these fish come out of the ocean to lay their eggs in the wet beach sand, in accordance with a most amazing and uncanny built-in clock. Indeed, a keen sense of timing is absolutely essential for their survival. Of all the varieties of fish in the world, only the grunion show such spawning habits. To understand some of the reasons why the sex life of the grunion is such a remarkable example of a "living clock," we need to consider some facts about ocean tides.

First, there are two low tides and two high tides roughly every 25 hours. Second, the highest tides occur at the time of the full moon and at the time of the new moon (at intervals of about two weeks). The grunion, with little variation, spawn at high tide on the second, third, and fourth nights after the full moon and after the new moon. This means that they are spawning after the time of the highest tides of the month (at a time when the high tides are declining). Sand is carried away from beaches when tides are increasing, so the grunion spawn on nights and at that time of night when tides are declining and their eggs will be covered by sand. If they spawned at that time of the month or at that time of night when tides were getting higher, their eggs would be washed away by succeeding tides and grunion would become extinct. Morever, since it takes about nine days for their eggs to develop, they must spawn at a time when their eggs will have nine days in the sand before they are washed free. Eggs which are laid on the second, third, and fourth nights following the highest tides will usually hatch from one to three nights before the next highest tide. But if the grunion were to spawn later than these three nights, their eggs would be washed out before they were ready to hatch.

Finally, it is essential that the eggs hatch within a few minutes after they are agitated, but not until they are agitated. If the eggs hatched as soon as they got wet, they would probably hatch pre-maturely and the baby grunion would die. In nature, the vital agitation comes when the eggs are washed free from the sand by waves of rising tides. Thus the grunion must take a multitude of factors into account in order to reproduce.

No one knows the exact mechanism controlling the precise timing of the grunion, but precise it is. Without this timing, they would have little chance of survival as a species. Yet how did the grunion acquire their incredible built-in clock? If they "evolved" their sense of timing over thousands or millions of years, the grunion would have long ago become extinct! Remember, the timing must be almost perfect; the eggs must be laid at just the right time - just after the highest tide for that month - otherwise the eggs would be washed away before they could develop. And the eggs must develop in nine days so they will be ready to hatch when the next highest monthly tide comes in. If they aren't ready to hatch, the tide will take them away and they will die. Truly the clockwork sex life of the grunion is an awesome spectacle. The grunion's incredible and intricate sense of timing is a powerful testimony to the handiwork of the Creator.

The Ant - by Mark Stewart

Surprising as it may seem, the tiny ant poses one of the biggest challenges to the belief that sex is a product of evolution and the survival of the fittest, or, on the other hand, that evolution is the natural result of sexual reproduction. One problem lies in the existence of sterile female workers in the ant community. Indeed, Charles Darwin, the father of the theory of evolution, was concerned that such neuter worker ants could be "actually fatal to the whole theory." In his 1859 book Origin of Species, Darwin stated: "With the working ant we have an insect differing greatly from its parent, yet absolutely sterile; so that it could never have transmitted successively acquired modifications of structure or instinct to its progeny. It may be asked, how is it possible to reconcile this case with the theory of natural selection?"

And that's precisely the point: These highly specialized workers differ greatly from their mother, father, and even from each other. Darwin observed that they differed by "an almost incredible degree." So one might assume they became specialized by evolution and natural selection over millions of years. But they're sterile! So they couldn't possibly have evolved by passing on characteristics to their offspring.

But could the queen ant, the mother of the neuter workers, be the source of their "evolution"? Modern-day evolutionists speculate that perhaps fortuitous mutations or sexual recombinations in the genes of ant queens gave rise to the remarkable variety of highly adapted workers we now find in ant colonies. After all, unlike the workers, queen ants are sexual creatures. Therefore, according to evolutionary theory, they might be expected to more readily evolve, introducing a wide variety of innovations in their offspring.

But the evidence simply does not support such speculations. Fossilized ants - males, females, and workers dated some 70 million years old - are apparently identical with species now living! Queen ants are a result of sexual reproduction. Yet the enigma is that sex, the presumed source of great evolutionary variety and change, has seemingly failed to effect any significant changes since the time of the fossilized ants. Sex or no sex, the evidence is that, regardless of the time period involved, the ant has not evolved. Surely the tiny ant provides a major challenge to Darwinian concepts of evolution.

Unexpected Art In The Ocean

Author Alexander Mebane is not a Christian or a Creationist. This is evident in the introduction to his book in which he writes,

> "... anti evolution writings reveal the rather dismaying fact that, historically, almost 90% of such publications have based their arguments on the axiom that reliable information is to be found in the creation myths of the ancient Hebrews. Let me make clear at once that this essay is not in that category! Today, no mind that has not been warped by childhood "imprinting" could find anything to take seriously in those naive and self contradictory old fables, whose absurdity became evident to unbiased minds some two centuries earlier than that of the later, more plausible creation myth of Darwin".

Yet Mebane recognizes the failure of Darwinism to explain much of what he observes in the natural world. The following is an excerpt from his writing.

> But the strangest of all "unnatural" natural beauty is that which is found beneath the sea. That seashells, for the most part, are exquisite works of art has always been known; the impression they force upon us is well expressed by the title of that lavishly illustrated 1988 volume by H. & M. Stix and R.T. Abbott, "The Shell: Five Hundred Million Years of Inspired Design". But it is only quite recently, since the advent of Cousteau's "scuba" apparatus, that the fantastic, multicolored beauty of the inhabitants of coral reefs, a province of "Nature" that, because hitherto inaccessible, still remains largely virgin and unruined by man, could be seen with our own eyes. And this beauty seems strangely paradoxical, for it could never have been seen by anyone until we contrived to bring our artificial lights down to it.
>
> Below a quite shallow depth, twenty feet or so, its brilliant red and yellow colors were never visible to any human or animal eye because that depth of water removes all but the blue from sunlight that strikes down through it. What a strange and incomprehensible finding that "Nature" should have provided so rich a spectacle of brilliantly contrasting hues, which nevertheless were in situ completely invisible until we brought our white lights down and revealed its secret! The ex-

> *planation that this wonderful feast of naturally invisible colors was provided by some benign Designer expressly for the delectation of late twentieth century humans seems too absurd to take seriously.*
>
> *But even more absurd (as I am sure no spectator can help feeling) is the Darwinist's explanation that all of this amazing hidden beauty was produced unintentionally, purely by accident. ... I cannot point to any "reasonable" resolution of these misgivings; I believe that no one could; but, speaking for myself, the manifest presence of aesthetic beauty in "Nature" is the only argument for the agency of a "God" that I have ever been able to take seriously.*

The Woodpecker - Mark Stewart

One of the most interesting sights you probably recall from childhood experience was a woodpecker hammering furiously against a tree. I have on a number of occasions. I have also seen hummingbirds. Anyone who has spent much time in the woods in almost any part of the United States has heard the familiar rat-a-tat-tat of a woodpecker banging his sharp, stout beak against wood. Woodpeckers have some of the most remarkable habits of all living things. They are another amazing example of highly specialized creatures who obtain their food in a very unusual manner.

One ornithologist told of seeing a woodpecker land on his favorite oak tree. Seeing the blurred head as the bird furiously hacked clouds of splinters and sawdust out of his favorite tree, the man shouted at the bird, then decided to girdle the part of the tree the woodpecker had attacked with a heavy mesh wire, in an attempt to discourage it. But the woodpecker was soon back. This time, the man found the wire mesh in shreds, and the bird busily drilling deeper into his tree! Finally, however, after finding the going a good bit tougher through the wire, and after being frightened away repeatedly, the bird was heard by the owner of the tree drilling away on trees more distant in the forest. Several years later, he reported, a severe storm snapped his beautiful oak tree right where the woodpecker had been drilling. Deep within the trunk, the ornithologist discovered a big colony of carpenter ants, and a labyrinth of galleries they gnawed inside it. It was then the man decided that, had he permitted the woodpecker to clean out that ant nest, he would still have his beautiful oak tree, only made more rustic by the familiar drilling marks of the bird families' answer to the jackhammer, the woodpecker.

But how did the woodpecker know those ants were deep inside a tough old oak? Why does a woodpecker obtain his food in the most difficult manner possible? Could woodpeckers have "evolved" gradually - learning to "survive" in the only way possible for them, pecking deep into tough trees?

There are many different species of woodpeckers. One hundred seventy-nine in the world, and twenty-two of them in North America. They range in size from the huge pileated woodpecker (19 inches from tip of tail to tip of beak - about the size of a crow) to the tiny downy. Each species finds its food in a slightly different fashion, and feeds on different things. The little downy feeds on caterpillars found in small twigs and tiny crevices, while the redheaded woodpecker (the one with which most people seem at least partly familiar) feeds on ants and grubs inside the trees. The gaudily decorated pileated woodpecker can strip the bark completely from a tree. One ornithologist watched a huge pileated woodpecker remove 30 feet of bark from a tree in less than 15 minutes! The tree had been attacked by carpenter ants, and the woodpecker's eradication of the ant colony prevented the spreading of the ants to other healthy trees nearby.

The woodpecker is totally different from other birds. First and most obvious is its beak. It is straight, very hard in comparison with most birds, and pointed. The head is constructed differently, too. The skull is much thicker than that of other birds, and the skull and beak are moved (sometimes more than 100 times a minute!) by powerful muscles. The bones between the beak and skull have their own built-in "shock absorbers", being constructed differently than those of other birds, which are usually directly joined together. In the woodpecker family, the beak and skull are joined by connective tissue that is spongy and elastic. Every part of the woodpecker's anatomy is specially constructed for the sole purpose of drilling into wood. Their claws are divided into two sharp and powerful toes forward, and two backward, like a pair of ice tongs, for gripping the bark. Their tail feathers act as a brace, steadying the bird on a firm tripod as it whacks away. The tail feathers are unusually strong, and during molting season, the main propping feathers don't fall out until other feathers have already been replaced and can support the weight of the bird while the bigger, stronger feathers molt.

How do they locate their food? Once, a pileated woodpecker was observed whacking away on a tough old hickory. Ants were using a little knothole as an entrance into the tree but the bird ignored the knothole. Instead it began pounding on the trunk as it slowly circled the tree - tapping, then pausing. Then it drilled its way into the very heart of the ant nest - five feet below the knothole the ants were using. Ornithologists speculate the woodpeckers use their acute sense of hearing (another remarkable part of their anatomical structure) to locate the insects either by hearing the insects, or else detecting the subtle differences in the sounds of the woods over insect channels, or both.

The woodpecker's tongue is perhaps its most remarkable instrument. In most cases, it is barbed, and about four times as long as the beak. The woodpecker shakes his tongue in and out of his beak like a snakes' tongue. In some species, the tongue is coated with a sticky substance, used as bait to catch ants. A woodpecker will drill into a tree, then shake out its long, sticky tongue, waiting until the ants, believing it to be a worm invader, swarm all over it. The woodpecker then whips the unsuspecting ants into his mouth. Three woodpeckers were being studied in a cage by ornithologists when they decided to attempt an experiment. The experimenters tried holding food above and behind the bird's heads, and were astonished when they whipped their tongues up over their heads, snatching away the food, without looking around, or turning their heads!

Every different woodpecker performs a special service in policing a balanced forest. Woodpeckers are the only creatures who spend most of their waking hours banging their heads against wood. They do this because of the role they seem to have been assigned in the living community: to glean insects from under the bark of trees.

But when did the very first woodpecker decide to peck wood? Think about it. Let's imagine the very first attempt of a woodpecker to peck wood. If evolution had occurred, then it had to start somewhere! What made that first would-be woodpecker peck wood? Was it necessary for him to survive? That hardly seems likely. Millions of other birds are still with us; and they obtain their food many other ways. The would-be woodpecker would have to have his strong beak, his long tongue, his acute hearing, strong neck muscles, a thick skull, viselike toes and stiff tail feathers for support before he could start! The first would-be woodpecker would have to have developed these things before he would be a woodpecker and if he already had these things he was already a woodpecker!! And yet this is essentially how woodpeckers survive, by pecking wood on trees and eating ants.

The woodpecker is a prime example of a specialized creature designed by an intelligent creator and cannot be explained logically in other terms.

A Problem With Mutations

What would you do for a machine that fixes itself when it breaks down? According to a report in New Scientist, 18 Oct 2003, all cells have a group of proteins that constantly survey their DNA looking for mutations and repairing them. Some repair proteins are known to move along DNA strands checking each base pair, but this is too slow a process to prevent mutations from building up. Scientists at the California Institute of Technology in Pasadena noticed that DNA that had been damaged would not allow electrons to flow along the strand. Is it possible that repair proteins might use electrical impulses to test DNA without having to move to each strand?

Sure enough, investigators found an iron-sulphur cluster in many DNA repair proteins that is able to do this. The scientists believe repair proteins can quickly test lengths of DNA by sending electrons along DNA strands between two repair proteins. If the electrons are blocked, the enzymes know there is damage somewhere between the two proteins and can identify the DNA to be repaired. So what we have in biology is a fleet of machines, including you and me, that are designed not only to replicate but to correct replication malfunctions when they take place.

This of course raises an interesting question in evolution theory. If genetic errors (mutations) are the means for evolution, why does DNA seem to be designed to defeat the introduction of errors? Mutations seem to be an unwanted aberration...not the road to progress. And who are mutations unwanted by, if not a designer who wrote a program to protect his creation.

Honey Bee Excess

It is well known by almost everyone that honey is a fundamental food source for the human body, whereas only a few people are aware of the extraordinary qualities of its producer, the honeybee. As we know, the food source of bees is nectar, which is not found during winter. For this reason, they combine the nectar collected in summer time with special secretions of their body, to produce a new nutrient - honey - and store it for the coming winter months.

It is noteworthy that the amount of honey stored by bees is much greater than their actual need. The first question that comes to mind is why do the bees not work less and produce just enough honey for their own needs? We suspect bees were designed to produce honey not only for themselves but also for human beings. Bees, like many other creatures, are dedicated to the service of man, just as the chicken lays at least one egg a day although it does not need it, and the cow produces much more milk than its offspring needs.

How Bee Hives Work

Bees must carry out numerous "tasks" in the hive and manage all of them with excellent organization.

Air Conditioning: Bees can easily be observed ventilating the hive. The entrance of the hive fills with bees clamping themselves to the wooden structure and fanning the hive with their wings. In a standard hive, air entering from one side is forced to leave from the other side. Extra ventilator bees work within the hive to push the air to all corners of the hive.

Defense system: Two guardians are always kept at the entrance of the hive. If a foreign substance or insect enters the hive, they act to remove it from the hive.

Sealing The Hive: Bees produce a substance called "propolis (bee resin)" with which they carry out the "embalming" process. Produced by adding special secretions to the resins they collect from trees like pine, poplar and acacia, the bee resin is also used to patch cracks in the hive.

Bacterial Defense: Propolis has the feature of not allowing any bacteria to live in it. How do bees know that this substance is ideal for embalming? How do bees produce a substance which man can only produce in laboratory conditions with the use of sophisticated technology and knowledge? How do bees know that a dead insect causes bacteria production and that embalming will prevent this?

It is evident that the bee has neither any knowledge on this subject, nor a laboratory in its body to learn to accomplish these tasks. There is no mechanical, undirected explanation for its behavior. The bee seems to have been designed to behave in this manner.

Bees construct hives in which 80,000 bees live and work together by shaping small portions of beeswax. The hive is made up of beeswax-walled honeycombs, which have hundreds of tiny cells on each of their faces. All honeycomb cells are exactly the same size. This engineering miracle is achieved by the collective work of thousands of bees. Bees use these cells for food storage and the maintenance of young bees.

Bees have been using the hexagonal structure for the construction of honeycombs since the beginning. Mathematicians say the hexagonal structure is the most suitable geometric form for the maximum use of unit area. If honeycomb cells were constructed in another form, then there would be areas left unused; thus, less honey would be stored, and fewer bees would be able to benefit from it. While they have the same volume, the amount of wax required for hexagonal cells is less than the amount of wax required for a triangular or quadrangular one.

Bees themselves surely cannot have calculated this result, obtained by man after many complex geometrical calculations. These tiny animals use the hexagonal form innately, just because they are taught and "inspired" so by their Creator.

The hexagonal design of cells is practical in many respects. Cells fit to one another and they share each other's walls. This, again, ensures maximum storage with minimum wax. Although the walls of the cells are rather thin, they are strong enough to carry a few times their own weight.

Cell angle is critical. By raising cells 13 degrees on one end, they prevent the cells from being parallel to the ground. Thus, honey does not leak out from the mouth of the cell. While working, worker bees hang onto each other in circles and congregate together in bunches. By doing this, they provide the necessary temperature for wax production. Little sacks in their abdomens produce wax. Bees collect the wax with the little hooks on their legs. They put this wax into their mouths, and chew and process it until it softens enough and to give it shape in the cells.

The construction of the honeycomb starts from the upper side of the hive and continues simultaneously in two or three separate rows downward. The honeycomb slices, which started simultaneously from different directions, are so perfectly arranged that, although there are hundreds of different angles in its structure, it seems like one uniform piece.

How can such a delicate calculation be done by thousands of bees? It is obviously irrational to assume that bees have solved this task by their own intelligence. So how do they achieve this? An evolutionist would explain that this event has been achieved by "instinct". The term "instinct" is simply a word we use for a behavior we don't understand. Bees are guided from a unique source and thus they successfully come to perform tasks which they otherwise would not be able to. It is not instinct, but a designed-in behavior. What these tiny animals do is implement the program that God has particularly set for them.

Flight Navigation Of Bees

Bees usually have to fly long distances and scan large areas to find food. How does a bee describe the location of the flowers to the other bees in the hive?

By dancing!... The bee returning to the hive starts to perform a dance. This dance, repeated many times by the bee, includes all the information about the inclination, direction, distance and other details of the food source that enable other bees to reach it.

This dance is a figure "8" constantly repeated by the bee . The bee forms the middle part of the figure "8" by wagging its tail and performing zigzags. The angle between the zigzags and the line between the sun and the hive gives the exact direction of the food source.

However, knowing only the direction is not enough. Worker bees also need to know how far they have to travel to collect the ingredients for the honey, so a bee "tells" the other bees the distance of the flower pollens by wagging the bottom part of its body and creating air currents. For example, in order to "describe" a distance of 250 yards, it wags the bottom part of its body 5 times in half a minute. This way, the exact location of the source is made clear in detail, both with respect to its distance and its orientation.

All of these examples reveal both the structural design of living things and the inexplicable orchestration of their behavior. Evolution theory, or any theory that leaves out a Creator, has no credible explanation.

CHAPTER 5

Geology And The Flood

First Salvo In The Scientific War With God

In the previous chapter, we reviewed the story of life, because life came before the fossil record according to both creation and evolution. However, it was the study of geology where the first arguments developed against belief in the Biblical God. Somewhat like the universe, the layers of rock and other features on the surface of our planet have led men to believe they must have taken a very long time to form. Men are puny. We're overly impressed by size and expanse and measure our creator, intelligent or not, against our own small ability. How long would it take me to dig the Grand Canyon? A long, long time.

In an important way, it was the Church's fault that the geologists of two centuries ago abandoned the Biblical Flood model and went off on their current tangent with its utter rejection of the Biblical story. Up until that time Christians had never seriously considered the implications of the Genesis account of the great flood, thinking it was just a story about a lot of rain. Therefore, the geologists of the time considered the Biblical model to be forty days and nights of rain and realized that was not enough water to flood the entire surface of the Earth, What a shame. They were operating under a complete misconception of what the Bible relates. As you will learn later in this chapter, Genesis tells us that the initiation of the flood was the opening of the fountains of the deep followed by rain, implying that subterranean water was the source of most of the flood waters. And so those early geologists rejected the Bible based on their ignorance of what it said, a lesson we might heed for ourselves.

In 1830 Sir Charles Lyell, the leading geologist of Victorian England, published his Principles of Geology, which showed from the study of rocks that 'creation' was a much slower process than would appear from the Bible. He suggested that it took not six days but many millions of years. Nearly thirty years later, Charles Darwin argued for abandoning the biblical view that God created separate species 'each according to its kind.' In many ways, Darwin was a disciple of geologist Lyell. As an aside, neither man was a scientist by qualifications. Lyell was a lawyer and Darwin a clergyman. nevertheless it was geologists who began the revolution against God. However, creationists also know geology, so it was more than the evidence itself that led men to study the rocks and interpret them wrongly.

The period from the American Revolution and on through much of the 1800's is often called the "Revolutionary Age". Certainly it was revolutionary in the political arena as evidenced by the overthrow of monarchy in America and in France and the subsequent grand experiments in republican and democratic rule. However, equally important in making it a revolutionary age were the changes in thought that accompanied these societal upheavals. This was a time characterized by free thinking and the rejection of established standards and authority. Unfortunately, the Church represented part of that authority, and a growing intellectual elite was bent on undermining it. Acceptance of the truth of the Bible became one of the casualties of the time. Consider one of the effects of the French Revolution as described in Funk and Wagnall's Encarta Encyclopedia.

> *"Anticlerical hatred found further expression in the abolition, in October 1793, of the Julian calendar, which was replaced by a Republican calendar. As a part of its revolutionary program, the Committee of Public Safety, under the leadership of Robespierre, attempted to remake France in accordance with its concepts of humanitarianism, social idealism, and patriotism. Striving to establish a Republic of Virtue, the committee stressed devotion to the republic and to victory and instituted measures against corruption and hoarding. In addition, on November 23, 1793, the Commune of Paris, in a measure soon copied by authorities elsewhere in*

> *France, closed all churches in the city and began actively to sponsor the revolutionary religion known as the Cult of Reason."*

In light of the anti-Christian undercurrent of the French Revolution, it is not surprising that the first seeds of doubt were planted by the soldiers of Napoleon Bonaparte as they campaigned in Egypt and re-discovered the remains of the ancient Egyptian civilizations. Two things seemed clear from their early investigation: (1) the Egyptian civilization seemed older than the Hebrew civilization casting doubt on the status of the Hebrews as the oldest civilization originating from Biblical Genesis, and (2) the Hebrews were strangely absent from Egyptian historical records, a finding hard to reconcile with the Bible's claim that the Hebrews spent 400 years as Egyptian slaves.

Simultaneous to the findings in Egypt, a young British aristocrat named Charles Lyell began to make a name for himself in the science of Geology. Although Lyell was formally trained as an attorney, his wealth enabled him to pursue the study of geology building on the previous ideas of James Hutton. Lyell's contention was that processes we see in action today caused all of the geological features we see in the earth, and he brought to the popular consciousness many examples of geological features which seemed to proved that the earth was much older than the few thousand years suggested by the Bible.

One of Lyell's most famous examples was Niagara Falls. Niagara Falls has eroded a gorge seven miles long from its original location. Lyell interviewed local residents and estimated that Niagara erodes the escarpment over which it falls at the rate of about one foot each year, and by simple arithmetic determined that the gorge has grown to its present length over the course of about 35,000 years (1 foot per year times 5,280 feet in a mile times seven miles equals 36,980 years). Lyell slyly pointed out, without directly saying the Bible was wrong, that the falls' origin seemed to be thousands of years before the creation of the earth. From this example and others, it became easy to extrapolate that the earth could be hundreds of thousands and even millions of years old. After all, the Biblical chronologies were no longer a limiting factor if you just stop believing them.

Lyell's evidences for an ancient earth inspired a young divinity student and amateur naturalist named Charles Darwin to speculate about the diverse forms of living things he observed. Perhaps, if the earth was millions of years old, the variations that Darwin observed in living species could have developed over millions of years from simpler species. Darwin published his speculations in 1859 as "The Origin of Species by Means of Natural Selection or Preservation Of Favored Races in The Struggle For Life." The work created considerable controversy culminating in a debate between Bishop Samuel Wilberforce defending the Biblical view and Thomas Huxley defending the Darwinian view. Huxley was reported as winning the debate, and that victory caused other defenders of Biblical truth to soften their criticism of evolutionary theory and even seek ways to assimilate it.

Many theologians came to believe that a good case had been made by men of science for an ancient earth and an evolution of life over long periods of time. The evidence was convincing enough for theologians who were unprepared to challenge the evidence for evolution scientifically. Anglican Charles Kingsley typifies church leaders who rushed to endorse Darwin and was quoted by Darwin in his second addition as writing, "It is just as noble a conception of the Deity to believe he created a few useful forms capable of self development into other needful forms." Kingsley was rewarded for his endorsement of Darwinism by being named a fellow of the Geological Society and said in his acceptance speech, "I feel how little I know and how unworthy I am to mix with the really great men who belong to it." Once church leaders had accepted the views of Lyell and Darwin, it became necessary to reinterpret the Bible to reconcile what the Word seemed to say with this new scientific view.

Since Lyell's geology interpreted geological features as being formed by currently observable processes, a global catastrophe such as Noah's flood was considered unthinkable, and theologians felt a need to explain the flood to skeptics. Dr. Samuel Turner of the New York Episcopal Church was one of the earliest to teach that Noah's flood was a local flood restricted to the Middle East in his "Companion to the Book of Genesis" textbook for seminary students, and Cardinal Nicholas Wiseman in England published a series of lectures expounding on the local flood concept. These interpretations survive today in spite of their obvious incompatibility with Scripture. Genesis 6:7 says, "So the Lord said, I will wipe mankind, whom I have created, from the face of the earth - men and animals, and creatures that move along the ground, and birds of the air - for I am grieved that I have made them." Genesis 6:17 continues the global theme saying, "I am going to bring floodwaters on the earth to destroy all life under the heavens, every creature that has the breath of life in it. Everything on earth will perish." The writings of the apostle Peter show that belief in a worldwide flood continued to the time of the Roman Empire. He writes in 2 Peter 3:5-6, "But they deliberately forget that by God's word the heavens existed and the earth was formed out of water and by water. By these waters also the world of that time was deluged and destroyed."

Yet a second compromise, this time to explain the long ages required by Lyell's geology, was the Day-Age theory introduced by Scotsman Hugh Miller. He proposed that the days of creation represented long periods of time citing "one day is with the Lord as a thousand years" in 2 Peter 3:8 as evidence. A similar attempt to expand the days of creation to allow for the long ages claimed by secular geology was the Gap or Ruin/Restoration Theory proposed by Edinburgh Professor of Divinity Thomas Chalmers. The theory claimed a gap between Genesis 1:1 and Genesis 1:3 with the Bible giving no details about the duration of the earlier period. During this period, pre-Adamic men and animals were destroyed in Lucifer's rebellion, the geological formations developed, and then the world was re-created beginning in Genesis 1:3. The gap theory gained influence when it was included in the Scofield Reference Bible. Yet both the gap theory and the day-age theory result in contradictions, not the least of which is Exodus 20:11 which says, "For in six days the Lord made the heavens and the earth and everything in them." Similarly Genesis 2:1-2 says, "Thus the heavens and the earth, and all the host of them were finished. And on the seventh day God ended his work." This clear statement of God's creative process leaves no room for a gap or long ages.

Theistic evolution, the idea that God used the processes of evolution, was the next attempt to reconcile 19th century science with the Bible. Asa Gray, a Harvard Professor of Botany who became Darwin's apostle in America, invented theistic evolution to make Darwin's theory seem less atheistic. Gray was quickly joined by Yale Professor of Geology James Dana and largely due to their efforts the previous largely Christian base of America's two great universities was converted first to theistic evolution and ultimately to atheism. Other theologians such as Pierre Teilard de Chardin, Catholic Jesuit priest, philosopher, and paleontologist, have influenced the major Christian denominations to largely accept evolution or at least deny that any conflict between the Bible and secular science exists.

Ultimately it became necessary for modern religious philosophers to explain how the early books of the Bible in particular could diverge so seriously from the teachings of science, and they did so by deciding that those early books are simply untrue. Julius Wellhausen in his Documentary Hypothesis proposed that the Bible's Genesis account was simply an adaptation by Jewish scribes of ancient Babylonian myths and legends. He based his claim on the "fact" that writing had not yet been invented at the time that Moses was supposed to have compiled the book of Genesis.

It may be hard for some Christians to believe that other Christians have moved so far away from the fundamental belief in the Bible as literal truth, so I am including this excerpt from a book I borrowed from the Camden County Library called *Is God a Creationist* with the subtitle *The Religious Case Against Creation Science*. The author writes:

> "When Christians like Asa Gray rejected the mechanical reading of scripture and accepted the different paradigm in which historic biblical religions would primarily develop, they did so in good measure because of Darwinian evolution, but also because of then current developments in biblical study itself. Even before the 19th century, new methods of historical research were introduced into the analysis of the Bible, its origin, growth, and content. As a result, it became increasingly apparent, on the basis of solid historical and archaeological evidence, that the Bible as we know it was itself formed through an evolutionary process. The Book of Genesis did not spring from Moses' pen but was apparently brought together from four independent documents."

We can see in this author's view that even the Bible is "evolving", but how do we reconcile this bit of wisdom with the many claims in scripture that God's word never changes. Psalm 111 verses 7 and 8 says, "The works of his hands are faithful and just; all his precepts are trustworthy. They are steadfast forever and ever, done in faithfulness and uprightness." Romans 1:25 speaks eloquently about modern man's rejection of the Word and belief that the natural world is all there is, "They exchanged the truth of God for a lie, and worshipped and served created things rather than the creator..."

So what can we conclude from this brief review of the beginnings of evolutionary theory and the church's attempts at compromise? Let's first consider the evidence for evolution that was presented in the century of Lyell and Darwin.

Twentieth century science has been unkind to the examples of long ages which Charles Lyell presented to the world a century earlier. Most geologists now accept that Niagara Falls is no more than 12,000 years old as compared to the 35,000 years claimed by Lyell, and even this modern view is subject to revision downward. A recent publication of Canada's division of tourism stated that the falls has been observed to be receding at the rate of five feet per year, an estimate which would reduce Lyell's 35,000 years to 7,000, considerably closer to the Biblical time for the flood. And if we note that considerably higher volumes of water immediately after the flood would result in faster erosion, it becomes easy to see Niagara beginning to cut its gorge between 4,000 and 5,000 years ago, precisely at the time of the flood.

Similarly, Darwin's central ideas have been largely discredited in the twentieth century as modern evolutionists have adopted such labels as neo-Darwinism to attempt to revise the theory to fit the facts. The science of genetics, unknown in Darwin's day, seems to indicate absolute limits which prevent one species from transmuting into another species as Darwin postulated. The variations Darwin saw within a given species were the result of genetic traits that already existed in the species, and science has yet to experimentally identify a way for new, constructive genetic information to come into existence.

Then there is the matter of the Egyptology that seemed to indicate discrepancies with Biblical history, but modern archaeologists are finding greater agreement than was first recognized. Archaeologist William F. Albright wrote, "The excessive skepticism shown toward the Bible by important historical schools of the eighteenth and nineteenth centuries has been progressively discredited. Until recently it was the fashion among Biblical historians to treat the patriarchal sagas of Genesis as if they were artificial creations of Israelite scribes. Eminent names among scholars can be cited as regarding Genesis 11 - 50 as reflecting late invention. Archaeologic discoveries since 1925 have changed all this. Aside from a few die-hards among older scholars, there is scarcely a single Biblical historian who is not impressed by data supporting the substantial historicity of the patriarchal tradition." Millard Burrows of Yale added, "Archaeology has refuted the views of modern critics. It has shown in a number of instances that these views rest on false assumptions and unreal, artificial schemes of historical development."

Oral history, one of the foundations of Wellhausen's Documentary Hypothesis has also been called into question. In 1973, a set of ancient tablets was found in Ebla showing that writing existed in 2300 BC, 1,000 years before Moses. The Ebla tablets substantiate Bible history by referring to all five cities of the plain in the same order as Genesis 14. Archaeologists have also found a written account of creation, once again refuting the notion that all information at this time was retained by inaccurate oral tradition.

There has been a renewal of interest in scientific creationism because 20th century science has proven 19th century evolutionists to have been wrong, and because the various compromises church leaders have introduced to reconcile discredited science with the Bible are scripturally unsatisfying. The popularization of evolution was not the result of compiled scientific evidence, but was based on the speculations and philosophical views of amateur science investigators. Yet it is significant how easily the great leaders of the church have been swayed to accept these speculations, and their experience should serve as a model and example for us. We simply mustn't make the same mistakes.

I Peter 3:15 exhorts us to "always be ready to give an answer to anyone who asks you to give the reason for the hope you have." How will we witness to the world at large and to our own children? When the world is teaching that life evolved and religion is a vain attempt to explain natural processes, can we be assured that our children will retain faith or that we can lead non-believers to believe? The answer is to equip ourselves with knowledge of God's world as well as God's word and to pass that knowledge on.

What Scientists Observe

The globe is covered by sedimentary rock primarily deposited by water. Those sediments are composed of horizontal bands that give the impression of deposition one layer at a time. I say "give the impression" because there are other ways to explain the banding. When sediments were deposited, animals and plants were captured in the sediments, and a fossil record left in the sediments.

Much of geological research spills over to living things because of those fossils. As a general rule, creatures buried deepest in rock layers (strata) are sea creatures. At the highest layer are the mammals. But it isn't just the depth in the layers that we observe. In fact, there is no place on Earth where we observe all the layers one on top of another. Different kinds of fossils are found in different regions. For example, dinosaurs are common in Colorado. Crinoids (sea creatures) are common in Missouri. At least one dinosaur has been found in southeast Missouri.

Geologists also have observed that continents seem to fit together. The fit suggests that the continents were once joined to form a single land mass. The theory of plate tectonics says that the Earth's crust is made up of moving plates that caused a past single continent to split into the several continents we have today.

Volcanoes concentrate in specific regions of the Earth's surface. The "ring of fire" circles the Pacific coastal region where most of the Earth's volcanoes and quakes occur. Volcanic rock contains radioactive elements. Scientists attempt to use radiometric decay rates to determine the age of volcanic rock and the sedimentary rock layers adjacent to volcanic rock.

Wind and water erode rock. Rock layers around the world are changed and sometimes completely removed by wind and water erosion. Present processes provide clues regarding how geologic features have been affected. Geologists try to reconstruct past events by extrapolating the effects of rock deposition, erosion, and the presence of fossils into a history of life on Earth.

We also know that geologic catastrophes happen. We may look at the Earth's surface as it is and imagine how observable processes like wind and rain operate, but we can't know simply from observing exactly how large-scale exceptional events in the past affected the planet. We can see that Earth has been shaped by extreme events like meteorite impacts, floods, and ice ages. Catastrophes make it difficult, if not impossible, to really know past details.

These are the things we observe. We might discuss other concepts like the makeup of the planet's interior, the core and the mantle and the crust, but those topics have little to do with our interest in the history of the Earth's surface.

Whatever story we read into geology is an interpretation of the surface features of the planet.

Evolutionary Geology

Modern geology (evolutionary, humanistic geology) tells a story about the observations. It's like one of those forensic detective shows on TV where a re-creation of the past is constructed from subtle clues. On TV, the construction of a case invariably leads to a confrontation with the suspect and confession of the crime. Unfortunately for geologists, the Earth never confesses what really happened.

The concept of uniformity is sometimes used to describe the regular processes of geologic history. The founders of modern geology assumed the present is the key to the past...that geologic formations resulted from processes similar to those we observe in the present. For example, Grand Canyon must have been carved by the Colorado River that we currently see flowing through it. Evolutionary geologists generally believe that rock strata (layers) are laid down a little at a time either seasonally or by infrequent, but recurring local floods. Deposition of Earth's strata required hundreds of millions of years, if you only allow for the processes we observe to produce it. If we assume those millions of years of processes alone, then fossil remains of dead creatures in those strata record evolutionary history. I mentioned a process bias in an earlier chapter. Early geologists had two basic observations...the existing strata and observable processes of rain and wind and tectonics. They rejected the Bible as a reliable historical reference document. Instead, they rely on figuring out processes.

The principle of horizontality asserts that rock layers are laid down horizontally. Geologists assume rock layers have been laid down one at a time in horizontal "blankets" in a sequence. Whenever strata is not horizontal, it must have been moved from its original position often by tectonic forces that bent or fractured the strata.

The principle of superposition is this. If horizontal layers form one at a time like blankets, the layer at the bottom must have been deposited first and is therefore the oldest. Layers on top were deposited on top of each lower level and are more recent than the layer below.

The principle of continuity extends these rules to a global scale. Strata that have similar content, both mineral and fossil, all around the world were deposited at the same time in geologic history. Based on this principle, a distinctive limestone layer dated as Triassic in Europe is the same age as a limestone strata found in North America even though they are thousands of miles apart.

Plate tectonics is a theory that Earth's surface is composed of moving plates. It is the movement of those plates that caused the original single land mass to split up to form modern continents. The fact that continent outlines tend to be a mirror image of other continents suggests they once fit together before the plates moved.

Geologic Time Scale

Long before radiometric dating, evolutionary geologists developed the Geologic Table with names of each age based upon an assumption of biological evolution and the types of fossilized creatures found in each strata. Here is a brief summary. The geologic column is a hierarchical chart composed of eons, eras, periods, and epochs. Most of the fossil evidence is in just three eras named Paleozoic (ancient life), Mesozoic (middle life), and Cenozoic (recent life). Sea creatures dominated the Paleozoic with the oldest period, the Cambrian, being about 500 million years ago (500 MYA) to the end of the Paleozoic in the Permian Period almost 250 MYA. The Mesozoic Era was the age of reptiles beginning with the Triassic Period less than 250 MYA and ending with the Cretaceous Period about 66 MYA. In case you're wondering, the Jurassic, of Jurassic Park fame, was sandwiched between the Triassic and Cretaceous. We live in the Cenozoic Era, in the Quaternary Period, in the Holocene Epoch.

It's hard for anyone not to reference the age-related classifications when discussing fossils and prehistoric life, even if you reject the millions of years aspect. Dinosaurs being from the Jurassic is just such a common thought. However, you can just think of the Jurassic as a type of strata where dinosaur fossils are found and not necessarily an age of history.

What Scripture Tells Us

Scripture doesn't give us direct revelation on the technical aspects of geology such as stratigraphy or the fossil record. Rather, the Bible gives us a historical description of a global catastrophe, the world-wide flood of Noah. The world-wide flood has been recorded by cultures all over the world. The events of the flood are recorded in the Bible as follows.

The story of the flood begins in Genesis 6 where Noah is told by God that a judgment is coming against the evil of mankind. God's plan is for Noah to build an ark to preserve representatives of land animals to be preserved. Genesis 6:14-16 records, "Make an ark of gopher wood: with cells make the ark; and pitch it inside and outside with pitch. And thus shall you make it: let the length of the ark be three hundred cubits, the breadth of it fifty cubits, and the height of it thirty cubits. And the door of the ark shall you set in its side: with a lower, second, and third story shall you make it." It's a big structure, most likely shaped like an enclosed barge with three decks. Genesis goes on to describe how the animals were brought to Noah and what the nature of the flood would be. Yes, it would rain for 40 days and nights, and casual observers who leave it at that are skeptical that the sky contains enough rain to flood the entire planet. But Genesis 7:11 reads, "In the six hundredth year of Noah's life, in the second month, on the seventeenth day of the month, on that same day all the fountains of the great deep were broken up, and the windows of heaven were opened." It's an important clue that rain was not the only source of water.

Genesis 7:19-20 goes on to establish that this is truly a global flood as it reads, "And the waters prevailed exceedingly on the earth; and all the high mountains that are under all the heavens were covered. Fifteen cubits upward the waters prevailed; and the mountains were covered." The waters covered the planet for a year until Noah, his wife, and their sons and daughters-in-law were finally able to leave the ark and start to repopulate the Earth.

We're not told explicitly how the Earth was affected, but we can imagine. Many of the geologic features resulting from the flood were not the result of long slow processes, but rapid catastrophic processes. Or as creationist Ken Ham likes to point out about the Grand Canyon, "Was it a little bit of water over a very long time, or a lot of water over a little time?" The Bible is not specific about the effects of the flood, but it is reasonable to believe the effects would be extreme and evident.

Which animals were on the ark? Genesis 6:19-20 reads, "And of every living thing of all flesh, two of every sort shall you bring into the ark, to keep them alive with you: they shall be male and female. Of fowl after their kind, and of the cattle after their kind, of every creeping thing of the ground after its kind, two of each shall go in to thee, to keep them alive." A qualification is added in verses 7:2-3, "Of all clean beasts you shall take by sevens, a male and its female; but of the beasts that are not clean two, a male and its female. Also of the fowl of the heavens by sevens, male and female; to keep seed alive on the face of all the earth." Only land animals had to be saved and only representatives of each kind, not every species and variety.

The Biblical Timeline

Beyond clues about Noah's Flood and geology, the Bible provides us with a framework for all things historical. Most people haven't studied Biblical Chronology, but it's important for everyone to understand the precision of the evidence of the Bible's timeline. Here is a timeline chart devised from *The Wonders Of Bible Chronology* by Philip Mauro. When was Noah's Flood? 2390 BC.

Person/Event	Explanation	Year of Man	Date BC
Adam	Creation of Adam	0	4046
Adam	Age at birth of Seth...130	130	3916
Seth	Age at birth of Enos...105	235	3811
Enos	Age at birth of Cainan...90	325	3712
Cainan	Age at birth of Mahalaleel...70	395	3651
Mahalaleel	Age at birth of Jared...65	460	3586
Jared	Age at birth of Enoch...162	622	3424
Enoch	Age at birth of Methuselah...65	687	3359
Methuselah	Age at birth of Lamech...187	874	3172
Lamech	Age at birth of Noah...182	1056	2990
Noah	Age at birth of Shem...502 (Shem	1558	2488

	was 100, two years after the flood and Noah was 600 at the time of the flood)		
Noah	Age at start of Flood…600	1656	2390
Shem	Age at birth of Arphaxad…100	1658	2388
Arphaxad	Age at birth of Selah…35	1693	2353
Selah	Age at birth of Eber…30	1723	2323
Eber	Age at birth of Peleg…34	1757	2289
Peleg	Age at birth of Reu…30	1787	2259
Reu	Age at birth of Serug…32	1819	2227
Serug	Age at birth of Nahor…30	1849	2197
Nahor	Age at birth of Terah…29	1878	2168
Terah	Age at birth of Abram…130 (Terah died at 205 when Abram was 75)	2008	2038
Abram	Enters Caanan at 75 (430 year sojourn of Exodus 12:40 begins here and ends at Exodus 1533 BC)	2083	1963
Abram	Age at birth of Isaac…100	2108	1938
Abram	Age when Isaac weaned…105 (400 years before the exodus per Genesis 15:13)	2113	1933
Isaac	Age at birth of Jacob…60	2168	1878
Jacob	Age at birth of Joseph…91 (Jacob was 130 when the second year of famine came per Genesis 47:9. Since Joseph was 30 when he went before Pharaoh, after 7 years of plenty and 2 of famine, he was 39. Jacob's age of 130 minus 39 gives Jacob's age when Joseph was born.	2259	1787
Joseph	Before Pharaoh (Genesis 41:46)	2289	1757
Joseph	Dies at 110 years old	2369	1677

Moses	Born 80 years before the exodus (430 years after Abram entered Caanan 1963 BC)	2433	1613
Moses	80 years old at Exodus	2513	1533
Joshua	Takes Israel into Caanan (Just after Moses dies at 120, 40 years after exodus)	2553	1493
Joshua	Divides land after 6 years of war	2559	1487
Joshua	Dies at 110 - Judges 11:26 says Israel occupied Heshbon for 300 years from 2552 to 2852. Working backwards from 2852; subtract 1 year in the wilderness, 6 years to divide the land, 8 years under Cushan per Judges 3:14, 80 years rest by Ehud per Judges 3:30, 20 years servitude under Jabin per Judges 4:3, 40 years rest by Barak per Judges 5:31, 7 years servitude under Midian per Judges 6:11, 40 years rest by Gideon per Judges 8:28, 3 years usurpation of Abimelech per Judges 9:22, 23 year judgeship of Tolah per Judges 10:2 for a total of 286 years. Joshua died 14 years after dividing the land.	2573	1473
Judges	End of the 450 year rule of Judges after Joshua's death...Acts 13:18-20	3023	1023
Saul	Reigns 40 years starting 3023	3063	983
David	Reigns 40 years starting 3063	3103	943
Solomon	Reigns 40 years starting 3103 and Kingdom is divided into Israel (ruled by Jeroboam) and Judah (ruled by Rehoboam)	3143	903

Kings of Israel and Judah	Lineage of the kings of both kingdoms can be traced to the Babylonian captivity beginning with Daniel and three friends	3519	525
Cyrus	70 Years captivity prophesied in Jeremiah 25:11-12 ends with decree to rebuild the temple	3589	457
Jesus	Born 30 years before year baptized	4041	4
Jesus	Baptized and anointed as Christ 483 years after decree to rebuild the temple in Jerusalem per Daniel's prophesy about 69 weeks of years (483 years) followed by the 70th week (7 years)	4072	27AD
Jesus	Crucified middle of 70th week	4075	30AD
Stephen	Martyred end of 70th week	4078	33AD

Creationist Geology - The Hydroplate Theory

Flood theorists have long wondered regarding the source of water sufficient to cover the entire Earth exceeding the tallest mountains as described in Genesis. A mitigating factor may have been an early Earth topography lacking in high mountains and deep valleys. A water vapor canopy in or above the atmosphere was proposed as a water source, but no theoretical model provides for enough water. There may in fact have been a canopy, but the canopy alone is insufficient to explain the flood. The Hydroplate Theory developed by Dr. Walt Brown focuses on a profound clue in Scripture, the fountains of the deep opening, coupled with our modern scientific understanding of plate tectonics.

Before elaborating on the Hydroplate Theory, let me make it clear that I am not "explaining away" the power of God with a materialistic substitution. God could have judged the people of Earth in a purely supernatural way, but He chose to use a flood of water. The job of creation scientists is to offer an explanation of the processes God may have used along with an assessment of how, in this case, the planet's surface was affected. God's will was done; we are merely investigating His method.

The Hydroplate Theory is a comprehensive explanation accounting for the origin of the following geological features and processes which are subjects of controversy within the earth sciences.

- Jigsaw Puzzle Fit of the Continents
- Mid-Oceanic Ridge
- Major Mountain Ranges
- The Grand Canyon and Other Canyons
- Continental Shelves and Slopes
- Ocean Trenches
- Ring Of Fire Volcano and Earthquake Region
- Glaciers and the Ice Ages
- Sedimentary and Metamorphic Rock Strata
- Comets and Meteors.
- Radioactive Minerals

The theory proposes a cataclysmic flood whose waters erupted from worldwide, subterranean, and interconnected chambers of water within Earth's crust, the fountains of the deep. Those chambers of water under the continental plates were under extreme pressure from the weight of the continents and tidal pumping caused by the rotation of the Earth in coordination with the way the ocean tides rise and fall. The flood began with a crack in the continental crust releasing the pressure of the subterranean waters and causing the initial crack to circle the Earth's crust. The waters under extreme pressures erupted into the atmosphere along with rocky sediments broken off from the fissure in the crust. Most of the water fell as rain in sufficient quantity to cover the Earth. Once the crack in the crust opened, tectonic plates began to slide away from each other rapidly sliding on the lubricating waters still left in subterranean chambers. When continental plates finally met resistance, they buckled forming mountain ranges and lowland areas perpendicular to the motion of the continents. At the conclusion of the flood, those mountain uplifts rose above the flood waters and caused the water to drain into the oceans as well as large continental lakes.

It's easy to see how the Hydroplate Theory accounts for the fit of the continents. The Mid-Oceanic Ridge, that is 46,000 miles long and wraps around the earth, is a remnant of the fissure from which the fountains of the deep erupted. The theory also accounts for major mountain ranges being roughly parallel to leading edge of the moving continents where they would first run into resistance from adjoining plates. Similarly, the ocean trenches tend to be parallel and adjacent to continental mountain ranges where a plate buckled downward. The famous ring of fire in the Pacific marks the area where sliding crustal plates have collided allowing hot magma from Earth's interior to escape to the surface.

A more subtle prediction of the theory relates to the Ice Age. The Ice Age began after the flood because the oceans were heated by tectonic and volcanic activity causing greater than normal evaporation. The cloud cover resulted in much greater precipitation than normal and cooling atmospheric temperatures leading to a cool-down of the planet. It's very similar to climate models that warn about modern global warming resulting in disrupted weather patterns leading to more extreme storms including snow blizzards.

Comets and meteors are actually pieces of the Earth that were expelled into space when the fountains of the deep erupted. They contain water and even organic material that originated on Earth at the time of the flood.

The most surprising prediction of the Hydroplate Theory is the formation of radioactive elements. Radioactive elements gradually decay into stable elements and would generally be gone, or at least greatly reduced, after billions of years of cosmic history. Nevertheless, we have radioactive minerals. Walt Brown proposes that stable elements in the Earth's crust were "ramped up" by tidal pumping in the pre-flood Earth to become radioactive. During the flood, the release of energy rapidly decayed some of those elements resulting in distorted age evidence. The possibility of creation and rapid decay of radioactive materials has been confirmed in laboratory experiments and could be reproduced by these unusual natural processes and events.

French geologist Guy Bertault also performed some interesting experimental work regarding the creation of sedimentary rock strata. Bertault performed flume experiments which demonstrated that flowing water deposited banded layers laterally rather than top down. In his experiments, the oldest rock layers were not the lowest layers, but rather all the layers nearest to the source of the flowing water. Bertault's research does not prove that all strata is formed this way, but might explain the apparent order of fossils in the strata as related to sorting by specific gravity during deposition instead of sorting according to evolutionary development.

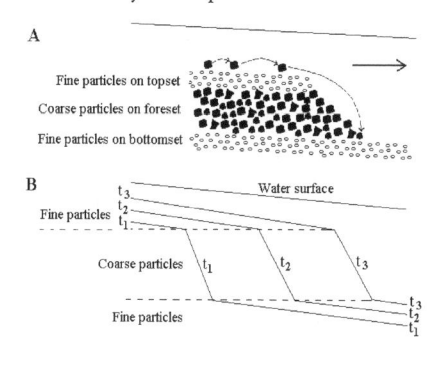

You can learn more about Walt Brown's geologic model at www.creationscience.com. Guy Bertault's theories are presented at www.sedimentology.fr.

Earth's Anomalies

Following are a collection of geological evidences that have great explanations from a Biblical creation point of view.

The Grand Staircase

Geologists refer to the southwestern United States from Grand Canyon across Arizona and New Mexico to the edge of California as the Grand Staircase. The region contains a staircase of rock layers from the bottom of Grand Canyon to the top of Bryce Canyon. Here is an illustrated cross-section of the rock layers in this region.

The Grand Staircase

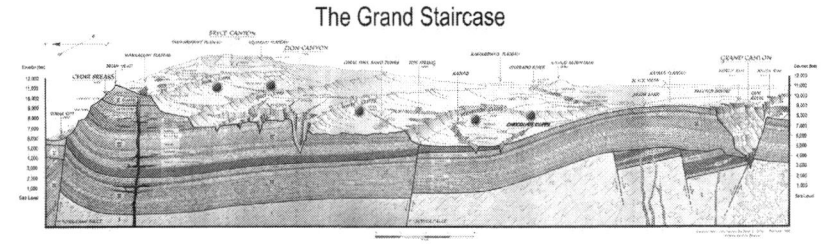

If we focus on the layer at the rim of Grand Canyon and follow it to the left (west) beyond Bryce Canyon, a significant observation becomes clear. There is a mile of layers above the Grand Canyon layer at Bryce. That mile of layers has been removed over much of the region. For tens of thousands of square miles, over a mile of sediment has been scoured away presumably by water, but none of these sediments have been found as deposits on the Pacific coast or in the Gulf of California. Where are those sediments?

The best explanation for the Grand Staircase is that flood waters covering an area the size of the North American continent washed the sediments away from the southwest and dispersed them so thoroughly that they can't be found. Any flood that would cover one continent would cover them all. Geologists have no better explanation, so many prefer not to talk about it.

Coal Formation

One of the good evidences for flood geology would be Dr. Steve Austin's work on the Kentucky No. 12 Coal bed, which was the basis for his doctoral thesis at Penn. State. The mainstream swamp origin theory for coal is challenged due to a number of items.

The material in the coal seams, when studied petrologically, contain rather large sheets of bark. This is in contrast to what is found in modern swamps where material is finely dispersed throughout the peat zone. These coal seams did not originate from a peat zone in a swamp, or from a peat bog, but had to have been deposited rapidly, buried, then coalified rapidly. (Coalification processes are short-time events rather than long time events, as demonstrated in lab studies.) Modern swamps destroy bark sheets by means of root penetration and other destructive processes. No paleosol zones underlie the coal seams. If coals, and their preceding peats, originated from growth zones, paleosols would be expected. This indicated deposition from transported material rather than in-place growth. This evidence is also found in many other coal deposits. The deposition model proposed by Austin has an uncanny resemblance to the situation found at Mt. St. Helens, Washington State. The log mat on Spirit Lake has deposited, on the bottom of the lake, similar kinds of material found in the Kentucky No. 12 coal seam. Austin's studies there have profound impact on interpretations of things like upright trees found in the fossil record with abruptly terminated root systems rather than in-place growth, which indicate violent uprooting with subsequent deposition. Austin's presentation of this material to many geological groups including the Canadian Society of Professional Geologists, perhaps one of the largest and most organized geological associations, was well received. In fact there was no real challenge to the evidences that he presented.

Flood Created British Isles

"Biblical Style Flood" made Britain, according to UK Daily Telegraph, 5 Sep 2006. Britain and continental Europe are believed to have been once connected by a series of chalky hills, but Britain became an island when these were eroded away. A sonar survey of the English Channel carried out by a team led by Sanjeev Gupta, from Imperial College, London, has revealed a huge valley containing "deep bowls, scour marks and piles of rubble on the sea bed that may have been caused by a torrent of water." Gupta suggests "the valley that now exists between Britain and Europe was created by a catastrophic flood following the breaching of the Dover Strait and the sudden release of water from a giant lake to the north." This could have made Britain into an island within 24 hours.

This research adds to the abundant evidence all over the earth of catastrophic processes, and it reminds us that massive geological changes do not need big time - they need big process. The movement of large masses of water can account for many landforms we now see on Earth, and it is interesting how deeply embedded the idea is that a catastrophic flood is a "Biblical style flood", an obvious reference to Noah's Flood described in Genesis as having destroyed the whole world in judgment of mankind's sin against God the Creator. (commentary by John McKay)

Mt. St. Helens

The eruption of Mt. St. Helens in 1980 was like a God-given laboratory demonstration for creationist concepts in geology. The explosive eruption caused a significant portion of the mountain peak to slide into Spirit Lake, displacing water to scour the mountainside, depositing a hundred feet of finely layered sediments, and eroding a miniature Grand Canyon in those sediments over the course of a few days. If scientists hadn't witnessed the events, they would have concluded that the layered strata had been laid down over thousands of years instead of just days.

Effects in Spirit Lake also gave geologist Steve Austin a new theory for rapid formation of coal. Thousands of trees were scoured off the mountainside and deposited in the lake where they floated horizontally for weeks. As the logs rubbed together, thick deposits of bark settled to the bottom of the lake. Then as the logs became saturated by water, they changed position and began to float in standing position root end down eventually sinking to the lake bottom in standing position.

As Austin examine these phenomena, he could see that the bark mats would eventually be transformed into coal underwater and proposed the floating mat model for coal formation at the conclusion of Noah's Flood. The new theory addresses many of the shortcomings of the standard peat bog theory for coal formation. He also noticed that the standing logs in Spirit Lake bore a striking resemblance to the petrified forests of Yellowstone. Those forests had been interpreted as being preserved where they grew and representing many different forest levels developing over thousands of years. Austin proposed that a bigger flood could result in uprooted trees being fossilized in standing position just like those in Spirit Lake.

The evidence at St. Helens is powerful because it takes all sorts of processes out of the realm of theory and shows us real results. Those results confirm that a world-wide flood would create the artifacts of today...Grand Canyons, fossil forests, and coal formations.

CHAPTER 6

Dragons And Dinosaurs

What Do We Know About Dinosaurs?

There have been some truly wonderful books written about dinosaurs. This chapter draws heavily on all of them, although I don't intend to just rehash old material. My wife tells me a little rehash is good, because a reader of this book may not have read the others. Regardless, I want to give special credit to two sources. First, there is Answers In Genesis in total and a couple of presentations by AIG speaker Mike Riddle. Riddle did a great job of drawing together diverse stories about dinosaurs and dragons while also refuting much of the evolutionary speculation. The second source I want to acknowledge is a wonderful pictorial book, Dire Dragons, by Vance Nelson. Calling it a "pictorial book" is misleading. Although it is visually stunning, Nelson is a diligent researcher who offers diverse and well-documented information.

What Dinosaurs Look Like

We see a lot of images of dinosaurs in books and movies and we forget that these are just educated guesses about how dinosaurs looked and behaved. All we really have are bones, and not even real bones...just fossils. Skeletal structures tell us something about the form of an animal, but you might be surprised what the bones don't tell you. Consider the skull of an elephant and you will see no trace of the elephant's famous trunk. The creature's most distinctive feature would be unknown if it wasn't for living elephants.

One Million Years BC was a movie from the 1960's. For its time, it reflected what people thought about dinosaurs and a common human desire to see dinosaurs for real. The movie made Raquel Welch a movie star. But let's use our imaginations to put our knowledge of Raquel in the same terms as the dinosaurs. Imagine we are aliens from another planet and we found all of Earth's people extinct and all we had were bones. Could we imagine what the soft parts of a human being looked like, the color of the skin, whether and where there was hair, finger and toe nails, etc. Could we really imagine a pretty girl like Raquel (because she'd even be pretty to an alien) or would we imagine a creature more like a gorilla?

Now think about a T-Rex. Did he have green skin? Was there hair on top of his head. Were there soft appendages like an elephant's trunk that the bones don't hint at? We may not know nearly what we think.

Varieties Of Dinosaurs

Identifying how many kinds of dinosaurs isn't a sure thing. Consider the changes that humans experience from childhood to old age. An infant and an old man look like entirely different kinds of creatures. There were many different looking but similar dinosaurs. Do some of these represent variations of the same animal? Think about the great variation among people...light skin and dark, straight hair or curly, pygmies and giants. Yet all are people. Dogs also show great variety from miniatures to Great Danes, yet all are dogs and can have puppies together.

Biologists consider two kinds of animals to be different species if they can't join to reproduce. The problem with dinosaurs is we will never know which varieties were capable of mingling reproductively. For example, could a male triceratops have a baby with a female eoceratops? Were they really the same kind with superficial variations. We can't tell just from their skeletons.

The Origin Of Dinosaurs

According to evolutionary speculation, about 220 million years ago, the first dinosaurs evolved from mammal-like reptiles or amphibians, long before man evolved. These creatures ruled the earth for millions of years and then became extinct. Many textbooks will site thecondonts as predecessors of the dinosaurs, but there are no actual transitional fossils between thecondonts and any dinosaur. If you go into any museum you will see fossils of dinosaurs that are 100% dinosaur, not something in between. There are no 25%, 50%, 75%, or even 99% dinosaurs-they are all 100% dinosaur! The alternate model is Biblical creation: all organisms created after their kind. All, including dinosaurs, lived concurrent with Man. It is sometimes said that the Bible is not a book of science. However, it is not a book of religion either. It is mostly a book of history and observation, both of which are elements of the scientific method. Note the assertion in Genesis that all animals reproduce after their kinds. Genesis records, "And God made the beast of the earth after his kind, and cattle after their kind, and everything that creeps upon the earth after his kind: and God saw that it was good, and the evening and the morning were the sixth day." Reproducing after their kind is precisely what scientists observe.

Dinosaurs And Time

Dinosaurs seem to be a universal source of entertainment for people of all ages; from very young children who idolize a friendly, purple monster named Barney, to children of all ages who love to be terrified by movies like Jurassic Park. And yes, people are even willing to be educated about dinosaurs as evidenced by the plethora of PBS specials featuring these amazing beasts.

But what do we know about dinosaurs? According to mainstream scientific theory, dinosaurs appeared about 225 million years ago and became suddenly and mysteriously extinct about 65 million years ago. Why did they pass away? A sign at the Natural History Museum in St. Louis proclaims that "one thing we do know is that man didn't cause the extinction of dinosaurs because dinosaurs and man didn't live at the same time." But do we really know what we think we know about these amazing creatures? When did dinosaurs live?

Dinosaurs live now! An intriguing animal called a Tuatara is a present-day native of New Zealand and represents a supposedly ancient line of dinosaur-like reptiles called beak-heads. Fossil creatures identical to the modern Tuatara have been dated by evolutionary paleontologists to be 200 million years old, older than most species of dinosaurs. Most scientists claim that the Tuatara survived in its present form because of environmental isolation from more modern creatures whose competition caused the beak-heads' extinction throughout the rest of the world. But why would none of the dinosaurs, many of whom could be considered more suitable for survival than the Tuatara, survive in the same environment?

That's a good question, for certainly if a 200 million year old Tuatara is alive today, any of the dinosaurs could have survived until relatively recent times and could have been contemporaries of Man. They could even be alive today, but undiscovered. Actually, the survival of dinosaurs until the modern era would explain a lot about ancient myths and historical records concerning unusual creatures. Understand, as a Biblical creationist I don't believe in the millions of years idea. The fact that the Tuatara is alive today is reasonable evidence that dinosaurs could have also lived recently and that extinctions didn't happen so very long ago.

What Do We Know About Dragons?

Are dragons really dinosaurs? There are two views about dragons. One idea about dragon stories around the world is that primitive people commonly make up stories about monsters. I guess that's possible, but there are also reasons not to believe that. After all, primitive people lived in proximity to so many real dangers, it hardly seems they would resort to made-up monsters to frighten themselves. There is also the question of why they would pick giant reptiles as their monster of choice unless they were inspired by real creatures. Modern reptiles just aren't big enough to inspire giant reptile legends. Finally, there is the question of why these dragon stories are so pervasive, appearing in many cultures around the world. It's one thing for one or two tribes to make up a story about dragons, but why would that be universal? The most credible explanation is that dragons are based on real experience. Furthermore, any mention of dinosaur-like animals prior to the 1800's discovery of dinosaurs is evidence that people saw dinosaurs in the past and called them dragons.

The people of northern Europe used the word "saedracan" to refer to reptilian creatures inhabiting oceans and lakes. I am reminded of dinosaurs like the plesiosaurs and tylosaurs. The book of Job describes Leviathan as a swimming reptile with scales and armor plating who can't be subdued by any man. This is obviously not a crocodile or alligator since we know men make shoes out of their hides. The land dragons of Europe were usually depicted as large reptiles with wings. We immediately think of the pterosaurs, but it could also be that the Europeans were seeing non-flying monsters with wing-like soft appendages that we wouldn't see in their fossilized skeletons. They also wrote about dragons breathing fire. Is that purely fantasy? The modern bombardier beetle has an internal mechanism for mixing two chemicals and directing hot gases explosively. We could also site the common firefly as a creature that can use chemical mixtures to produce light. Perhaps dinosaurs had similar features. Parasauralophus was a crested dinosaur with elaborate nasal chambers whose function is the source of speculation among dinosaur researchers. Perhaps they mixed chemicals in their sinus and nasal cavities to produce light and heat similar to the bombardier beetle. Just maybe there is a basis in fact for fire-breathing.

The Bible's Book of Job also famously records information about a dinosaur-like animal called Behemoth. We read in Job 40, "Behold Behemoth, which I made as I made you; he eats grass like an ox. Behold, his strength is in his loins, and his power in the muscles of his belly. He makes his tail stiff like a cedar; the sinews of his thighs are knit together. His bones are tubes of bronze, his limbs like bars of iron. He is the first of the works of God; let him who made him bring near his sword! For the mountains yield food for him where all the wild beast play. Under the lotus plant he lies, in the covert of the reeds and in the marsh. For his shade the lotus tree covers him the willows of the brook surround him. Behold, if the river is turbulent he is not frightened; he is confident though Jordan rushes against his mouth. Can one take him with hooks, or pierce his nose with a snare?" I can imagine that passage being a description of a dinosaur like apatosaurus or brachiosaurus or diplodocus.

Whereas Job is the oldest Biblical record of dragons, the story of Gilgamesh is equally old. Gilgamesh was a historical king of Uruk in Babylonia, on the

River Euphrates in modern Iraq. He lived over 2,000 years B.C. Many stories and myths were written about Gilgamesh, some of which were written down in the Sumerian language on clay tablets which still survive. These Sumerian Gilgamesh stories were integrated into a longer poem, the fullest surviving version derived from twelve stone tablets, in the Akkadian language, found in the ruins of the library of Ashurbanipal, king of Assyria 669-633 B.C., at Nineveh. In that epic story, Gilgamesh slays a dinosaur-like dragon. Both the Bible and "secular" histories therefore confirm that dinosaurs and man lived at the same time and had encounters.

There have been many more modern historical accounts of large dinosaur-like creatures. Pliny wrote in, Natural History, about 70 AD, "Africa produces elephants, but it is India that produces the largest, as well as the dragon..." The ancient Sumatrans produced multiple pieces of art depicting long-tailed, long-necked creatures with a head crest. Deep in the jungles of Cambodia are ornate temples and palaces from the Khmer civilization. One such temple abounds with stone statues and reliefs. These depict familiar animals like monkeys, deer, water buffalo, parrots, and lizards. However, one column contains an intricate carving of a stegosaur-like creature.

A mosaic that was one of the wonders of the second century world called the Nile Mosaic of Palestrina, depicts Nile scenes from Egypt all the way to Ethiopia. Scholars now believe this is the work of Demetrius the Topographer, an artist from Alexandria who came to work in Rome. The top portion of this remarkable piece of art is generally believed to depict African animals being hunted by black-skinned warriors. In one portion they are pursuing what appears to be some type of dinosaur. The Greek caption above the reptilian animal reads Krokodilopardalis which is literally translated Crocodile-Leopard.

Beowulf is a literary work from the Middle Ages relating the adventures of a hero in defeating a dragon. Many people don't realize that Beowulf was a historical person beyond the legend. The monster was called "Grendel", but that may have been not so much a name as a description. The word is derived from an Old Norse word for storm or bellowing. The book says that Grendel had the shape of a man but twisted or distorted. Grendel was also described as walking on two legs, that he killed with jaws and teeth, but that he had curiously weak arms. Beowulf broke those arms to defeat Grendel. Just maybe Grendel was a small Tyranosaurus rex-type of dinosaur.

Texas creationist Joe Taylor offers a cast at the Mt. Blanco Fossil Museum of Peruvian Ica stones bearing depictions of dinosaur-like creatures. In 1571 the Spanish conquistadors brought back stories that there were stones with strange creatures carved on them found in a region of Peru. These stones were produced long before the modern "discovery" of dinosaurs. Today, over 1100 such stones have been found by Dr. Javier Cabrera. In the early 1930's, his father found many of these ceremonial burial stones in Ica's numerous Peruvian tombs and noted that dinosaur-like creatures were represented on some of them. Skeptics claim they are forgeries because modern copies were being made and sold to tourists, but the stories of the Spanish explorers suggest that some of the stones are authentically old.

Even more intriguing are the stories of dinosaur-like animals surviving to recent times. Sea monsters were often reported during the age of ocean exploration around the time of Columbus. Many of these creatures are described as serpents but could also be similar to the long-necked long-bodied reptiles like tylosaur and plesiosaur dinosaurs. Those reports inspired writers like Jules Verne to popularize them in novels. But such reports continued right up to the first World War when U-boat Capt. Georg von Forstner reported on July 30, 1915, "The steamer sank quickly...When it had been gone for about 25 seconds, there was a violent explosion. A little later, pieces of wreckage, and among them a gigantic sea animal...was shot out of the water... It was about 60 feet long..."

Then we have the ropen of Papua New Guinea, described as giant flying reptiles. Papua New Guinea, or PNG, is a large island nation comprised of many tribal peoples where ropen are part of their folklore. Because of the mountainous terrain and isolated tribal regions, finding and documenting living ropen has proven to be an elusive goal. But the stories are intriguing, and similar sightings have been reported in Mexico and South America.

As I write this, I am realizing how tempting it is to drift back and forth between dinosaurs and dragons. Am I talking about dragons being real, or dinosaurs being modern? The two types of creature are so similar they must be the same. So let's try to map dragons to dinosaurs in the next section.

Which Is Which

If dinosaurs and dragons are the same animal, we ought to be able to match up a dragon type with a dinosaur variety. Obviously, we need to keep in mind that descriptions of dragons have been embellished by storytelling mixed with the terror of the storytellers who witness these creatures. Therefore, be gracious as we map each dragon to its dinosaur counterpart.

Saedracan To Plesiosaur

Among the dragons were creatures that were known to the Saxons and Danes as giant saedracan (sea-drakes or sea-dragons), and these were seen from the cliff-top suddenly swerving through the deep waters of the lake. Perhaps they were aware of the arrival of humans. Other creatures were lying in the sun when Beowulf's men first saw them, but at the sound of the battle-horn they scurried back to the water and slithered beneath the waves. The saedracans immediately bring to mind the monster of Loch Ness in Scotland. Their counterpart in the dinosaur kingdom is something like the plesiosaurs, extinct predatory marine reptiles that evolutionists place in the Triassic period of geologic time continuing into the Jurassic and Cretaceous periods. Fossilized skeletons of them have been found in North America, Europe, and Australia. The plesiosaur had a small, short head, a long, snakelike neck, a broad, solid body, and a short tail. Its sharp interlocking teeth were well equipped for catching fish, and its four paddle-like legs were similar to those of a marine turtle. In total length, Plesiosaurus ranged from 10 to 60 feet. The term plesiosaur is sometimes applied more generally to all forms in the order Sauropterygia, which produced two lines of marine reptiles.

Leviathan To Tylosaur

Leviathan is described in chapter 41 of the Book of Job as an aquatic monster that can't be captured with a hook. He is completely untamable and has double jaws containing horrible teeth and an armored body. Verse 22 asserts, "On earth there is none like him." His counterpart among the dinosaurs may well be tylosaurus. This marine reptile from the mosasaur family would have been a dominant predator. It had powerful jaws filled with large cone-shaped teeth. A smaller set of teeth in the roof of its mouth were used for swallowing prey whole.

European Dragon To Pterodactyl

European dragons were typically described as being able to fly, but also often were depicted walking on four legs. Perhaps these were two different monster creatures whose descriptions were blended into one due to the panic of terrified observers. But let's go with giant pterosaurs as the probable dinosaurian. A Pterodactyl had a wingspan of anywhere from a few inches up to over 40 feet. Pterodactyls are believed to have flown long distances using large wings, and they probably had above average eyesight to help them catch their prey. Paleontologists classify Pterodactyls as flying reptiles and not dinosaurs. According to old earth scientists, Pterodactyls lived in the late Mesozoic period, about 251 to 65 million years ago. Their diet was carnivorous. The fossils of Pterodactyls have been found in America, Europe, Africa and Australia. Just as an aside, flying reptiles aren't completely unknown today. There are about 15 species of gliding lizards in Southeast Asia. Most are about 8 inches long. On either side of the lizard's body are thin, wing like folds of skin supported by five to seven ribs that extend from the body. With its "wings" extended the lizard is capable of gliding for distances of up to 30 feet. The wings are often brightly colored, sometimes with stripes or spots. Flying dragons, as these lizards are sometimes called, have slender legs, tapering tails, and brilliantly colored throat sacs, typically blue in the female and yellow-orange with a blue spot in the male. They live in trees, rarely descending to the ground, and feed on arboreal ants. They are classified in the Class Reptilians, order Squamata, and family Agamid. It's interesting that their flying ability did not require true wings, but rather rib extensions. Perhaps dinosaurs that were not true flyers like the pterodactyls, were capable of gliding with rib extensions or cartilage and soft tissue that might not be preserved in fossils.

Chinese Dragons To Sauropod Dinosaurs

Chinese dragons are most often depicted like four-legged sauropod-style dinosaurs, although embellished with vivid color and stylized fins and crests. They are characterized as benevolent animals, and ancient Chinese legends claim they were used as beasts of burden, kind of like elephants. Sometimes the legs get lost in Chinese art, so they may also have had experience with creatures like the European Saedracan-plesiosaur having a more snake-like appearance. Sauropds include primarily herbivorous dinosaur varieties including brachiosaurus, diplodocus, and apatoaurus, therefore their benevolent nature and possible use as work animals is more credible than it would be if they were carnivorous varieties.

Were dragons and dinosaurs the same animal? There's no way to know for sure, but an interesting discovery just a few years ago provided new evidence for the claim. A new variety of dinosaur dubbed Dracorex hogwartsia was excavated in South Dakota. The name was inspired by a dragon in the Harry Potter series and means "dragon king of Hogwarts". The skull of Dracorex hogwartsia features elaborate horns and frills and an elongated snout that is very reminiscent of dragon depictions. Signage of a display at the Children's Museum Of Indianapolis points out the similarity of the dinosaur to dragon art. Maybe animals like Dracorex lived in proximity to humans and inspired both the history and the fanciful imagery associated with dragons.

CHAPTER 7

The American Experiment In Biblical Government

Give Us A King

The Lord Jesus was born into an interesting time in history, with many parallels to our own day. He brought to the world a new way to know God, directly and personally, without the intervention of an elite leadership priesthood. However, in opposition to that spiritual direction, the Romans were turning politically from the republic's citizen rule through a senate and embracing the cult of the ruling leader through the Caesars. That political direction is reminiscent of something the Hebrews went through in the days of Samuel.

Humanity seems to have an intuitive desire for a "great leader", a king. So it was with ancient Israel in the era when they were guided by judges who heard from God. The Judges weren't leaders like the kings who followed them. A judge was simply a conduit for the Hebrew people to hear from God. It wasn't enough. The people of Israel demanded from Samuel the prophet that they have a king like all the other nations. God replied to Samuel saying (and I paraphrase), "They have rejected me as their leader. They would rather be under the authority of a man. They want a king; I will give them a king, and then they will learn what happens to them under man's authority."

So Saul was chosen to be king and proceeded to do things his way rather than God's way. The prophet Samuel, a subordinate to Saul in human terms, continued to hear from God and obediently tried to bring Saul back to submission to God, but Saul was unable to receive it. Therefore God withdrew His anointing from Saul and called David, who was respectful of Saul as God's chosen man but nevertheless participated in Saul's eventual destruction because of his own calling from God.

But that's not the whole story. Even though David was a man after God's own heart, he perpetrated an atrocity by taking Uriah's wife, Bathsheba, and arranging with his soldiers to withdraw from the front lines so that Uriah would be killed. The men who participated in the murder of Uriah are representative of those men who are fully yielded to man's authority (the king) rather than God's. Fortunately for David, God's anointed, there was a prophet named Nathan who was obedient to God and presented to David a story about the killing of a pet lamb that was analogous to David's crime against an innocent man. King David became convicted that he had sinned, repented, humbled himself, and became reconciled to God in part through the obedient intercession of Nathan who obeyed God in bringing correction to the king.

The spiritual revolution that Jesus started was to subjugate man's rule, even the rule of holy men, underneath every man's personal relationship with God. Thanks to the work of Jesus Christ, each of us has a special calling from God. There is no hierarchy in God's kingdom. We all have a role to play and to be yielded to one another. King David was right in allowing God to use Nathan for correction. The clear teaching of scripture is that God's authority is superior to any man-based authority even when the man has been called by God as King David was.

The other moral of the story of David and Saul however, is that man's desire for a king and a king's desire for power runs deep. Julius Caesar came along as a charismatic leader and captivated the hearts of Rome leading to the institution of the "office" of Caesar with absolute power. The republic was overthrown, but more importantly, the Roman style of rule became the model for government for all of the centuries leading up to the American Revolution. The founding fathers of the United States contended with the despotic King George and decided enough was enough. But these were learned men, most of them Christian. They saw no purpose in overthrowing one king to simply replace him with another. What they determined was a revolution in the political realm that mirrored the spiritual revolution of Christianity. Political authority would return to the people under God, just as spiritual authority had.

Now more than 200 years after the revolution, the cult of leadership threatens the greatest political advance in mankind's history. Our cult of leadership involves the expansion of presidential power in opposition to our Constitution's expression of power vested in the people. It's all about worldview. Will government be rooted in the humanist subservience to other men, or the Biblical model's power to the people through individual responsibility.

The Founders Brought Forward: It's Worldview Again

The current conflict in American politics parallels the way Americans are conflicted about the Bible. As we read the Bible, it doesn't quite line up with what we want to believe, so we imagine that the Bible really says something else. That way we never have to confront our unbelief. Similarly, politicians want to accomplish tasks that are clearly not authorized by the Constitution, so they call the Constitution a "living document" that they and the courts can reinterpret to the point of ignoring its plain meaning.

A Letter To The Editor – Lake Sun Leader 2013

> *I don't usually respond to letters to the editor unless I think that I can offer something positive rather than just argumentative. A recent letter writer suggested that the federal government's Congress will just be "business as usual" featuring the same corrupt practices while another opined that reading the Constitution was simply a waste of time. I think these two opinions are closely intertwined even though they may come from opposite ends of the political spectrum.*
>
> *The reason we are so skeptical of federal politicians is that they have ignored the Constitution for so long that they are now effectively above the law. They tend to either be wealthy, privileged people or they will become such by taking advantage of their position of extraordinary influence and power. Liberal judges and the university academics who spawned their philosophy have repeated the assertion that the Constitution is irrelevant because the framers could not anticipate the nature and demands of modern society, but they*

conveniently ignore the fact that the framers provided an amendment process so that subsequent generations could modify the Constitution as needed to address changing conditions. The reason that liberals have not used the amendment process is that they know they couldn't convince enough Americans to make the changes that liberals want. Their workaround strategy is to ignore the Constitution while promising to uphold it.

Consequently, members of Congress feel no constraint to consider Constitutional authority before doing whatever they want to do. They are unaccountable. They simply interpret the Constitution rather than uphold the letter of the law which they swore an oath to uphold. The reading of the Constitution in Congress last week was a bold move intended to remind members of Congress of their ethical obligation to uphold the law of the land. Every session of Congress should open with a reading of the Constitution. The opinion that this was a waste of time has some merit because many members of Congress will simply not get it. They have never considered the Constitution while crafting legislation and asserting their power, so why should they start now?

What I would suggest is that this is a new day. It is not just like last year or ten years ago or any other time. We have now elected a group of Constitutional zealots who care more about the rule of law than acquiring personal power. I am hopeful that these men and women will stand firm as public servants instead of as politicians. There is always a risk that they will fail, but we should not fatalistically condemn them to premature failure. Rather we should support them with our prayers, our confidence, and our commitment to watch their backs as they confront the establishment.

A side issue in one of those opinion letters was the thought that the Federal government should shut down other programs and provide free health care for everyone. That is a kind-hearted wish, but not the right answer. Our problem with Congress is the size and power of the Federal government. That's why we feel so powerless as individuals to stop the corruption. Whether the Federal government becomes big by fighting illegal wars or by creating massive regulatory bureaucracy or by administering everyone's doctor visits, it will be too big for its citizens to control. An essential aspect of making Congress, the President, and the courts accountable to the people is to reduce the scope of the Federal government and transfer power back to state and local government. If citizens want health protection, do it at the state level where citizens have better access to oversight. At least then if state government makes a mess that can't be repaired, you can move to another state.

If there is any hope to restore the republic and to defend individual liberty, it is to remind people of how American government was designed to work. Keep power as local as possible where the citizens can monitor and control it. Simultaneously, keep distant government limited so that it can't be abused. – Bill Mundhausen

Biblical Government Equitable For All

Somehow, the reality that the United States was established on a Christian Biblical foundation has become controversial in recent years, in spite of the overwhelming evidence that it is so. I suppose it is because atheists feel somehow left out by the assertion. Is it really necessary to feel that way? Surely one can appreciate the historical reality of America's Christian beginnings even if they aren't Christians.

Perhaps Thomas Jefferson is the best example of what was going on with the founders, and is an example of how the gap between secularism and God-worship can be bridged. All of the founders grew up in the context of a Christian culture, but they were educated well beyond today's standard. They read classical literature and philosophy and considered the Bible a work that every educated person should read and comprehend. Their search was for principles that are effective regardless of the source, and they drew wisdom from Christian and secular sources alike. Jefferson was not a devout churchman, but he was far from an atheist, famously asserting that all men are created and endowed by their Creator. Jefferson was uniquely able to re-direct the truths of the Bible into practical application to govern believers and non-believers equally.

The 5,000 Year Leap

I already mentioned how the founding fathers of the United States were learned men who sought an alternative to monarchical government. They scoured classical literature and the Bible to identify the principles that would make sound government stable and just. The 5,000 Year Leap by Cleon Skousen was one scholar's attempt to summarize those principles. Skousen asserted that these God-honoring governing principles are the factor which enabled Americans to generate more financial and technological prosperity than the previous 5,000 years of history.

Principle of Liberty #1

"The only reliable basis for sound government and just human relations is Natural Law," wrote Cicero 106-43 BC. "True law is right reason in agreement with nature. It is unchangeable and constant. It recognizes God as a master and ruler who ought not be ignored. It is available to man via reason." Cicero was neither Christian nor Jew, but as a reasoning man knew the existence and sovereignty of God. I like to think of natural law as the normal consequences of an action. For example, being a thief is undesirable because your action damages the trust in commerce between people. When law is based on natural consequences, it seems intuitively fair, and the perception of fairness is a vital ingredient for public acceptance.

Principle of Liberty #2

Ben Franklin wrote, "Only a virtuous people are capable of freedom. As nations become corrupt and vicious, they have more need of masters." This is the fatal flaw in conservatism, libertarianism, and constitution advocates. America's problems are not just political. America's moral decline is at the heart of our political issues.

Principle of Liberty #3

"The most promising method of securing a virtuous people is to elect virtuous leaders." Americans began to lose this concept in earnest with Bill Clinton and the Lewinsky affair. That's when we said out loud that personal character was not a qualification for the Presidency. You can do the job even without a moral code. From there we got the Survivor reality show where the winner gets a million dollars by lying to and betraying his or her allies. It's art imitating life and life imitating art.

Principle Of Liberty #4

"Without religion (true religion) the government of a free people cannot be maintained." Why so? Christianity provides an external standard that regulates every believer's intended conduct. We reject bad behavior without the need for human laws. Without such a standard, godless men do whatever they wish and routinely violate the rights of others. They literally cannot live free without causing harm, which leads to the need for government to exert more and more control to restrict freedom.

Principle of Liberty #5

"All things were created by God, so upon him all mankind are equally dependent, and to him they are equally responsible." If we were only evolved animals, how could we claim that any intrinsic rights are due us? This is the great truth that men like Thomas Jefferson identified when he wrote, "We hold these truths to be self-evident, that all men are created equal; that they are endowed by their Creator with certain unalienable rights...." Creation is not a religious premise, but a sociopolitical necessity if we are to live as free men in peace with one another in a condition of liberty.

Principle Of Liberty #6

"The Founders knew that in these three ways, all mankind are theoretically treated as equal before God, equal before the law, and equal in their rights. " When government carves out a class of people (whether rich or poor) for special treatment, then government violates this principle.

Principle of Liberty #7

The proper role of government is to protect equal rights, not provide equal things. The founders recognized that the people cannot delegate to their government any power except that which they have the lawful right to exercise themselves. What does that mean? We can't give government the right to take whatever it wants, violate privacy, or harass individuals for political reasons. Government must operate within the law. Redistribution of wealth violates this principle.

Principle of Liberty #8

Men are endowed by their creator with certain unalienable rights. Unalienable means those rights are inherent, an essential aspect of Man that can't be rejected or transferred to a government, institution, or collective. This is only true if God is real. It's an indefensible proposition otherwise.

Principle of Liberty #9

God has revealed certain principles of divine law, but the laws of government are essential to protect rights. Rights, though endowed by God, could not remain unalienable unless they are protected as enforceable rights under a code of law. This is why the violation of laws is most egregious when government itself violates the law.

Principles of Liberty #10

"The God-given right to govern is vested in the sovereign authority of the whole people." We all learned about the "divine right of kings" when we were kids in school, the idea that dictators and monarchs had a privileged position ordained by God. It's a false idea. The God of the Bible treats every individual as sovereign over their own lives. By extrapolation, all of our individual sovereignty can be channeled to collective action. Therefore, don't try to delegate your authority to any one man or government. In human affairs, we don't need to be led. We need to lead.

Principle of Liberty #11

"The people may alter or abolish a tyrannical government. When a long train of abuses and usurpations evinces a design to reduce them under absolute despotism, it is their right and duty to throw off such government." If this post doesn't get me on a list somewhere, I don't know what would. Nevertheless, this is what the founders of America believed.

Principle of Liberty #12

James Madison wrote, "The United States Of America shall be a republic. Democracies have ever been spectacles of turbulence and contention; have ever been found incompatible with personal security or the rights of property; and have been as short in their lives as they have been violent in their deaths. A republic, a government in which the scheme of representation takes place, opens a different prospect and promises a cure for which we are seeking." We often hear politicians refer to our government as democratic. We even have a political party named after democracy. But the founders wanted to protect us from democracy through representative government. A pure democracy in which 51% of the population rules over the 49% remains perpetually undecided about certain issues. Furthermore, the 51% might have been influenced by deception. A limited number of representatives are more likely to be fully informed on an issue, and they are always subject to accountability and recall if they violate the public trust.

Principle Of Liberty #13

A constitution should protect the people from the frailties of their rulers. Madison wrote, "If angels were to govern men, neither external nor internal controls would be necessary...but lacking these you must first enable the government to control the governed; and in the next place oblige it to control itself." This is why adherence to the Constitution is a vital principle.

Principle if Liberty #14

Life and liberty are secure only so long as the rights of property are secure. The purpose of property rights is to ensure that the value of building on and improving the land is protected. Who will build if what they build can be taken from them?

Principle Of Liberty #15

Prosperity most follows a free market economy and minimum government regulation. Prosperity depends upon a climate of wholesome stimulation characterized by (1) the freedom to try, (2) the freedom to buy, (3) the freedom to sell, and (4) the freedom to fail. When politicians interfere with any of these freedoms, unintended consequences manifest that limit prosperity.

Principle Of Liberty #16

"The government should be separated into three branches: legislative, executive, and judicial." Have you noticed how the media is urging you to be dissatisfied with "gridlock"? This is progressivism wanting you to want "progress". Actually, gridlock is a good thing. Our system is designed to prevent any one branch from exerting too much power. Dispersion of power is accomplished by dividing the power among the branches. When the President complains about Congress, he is expressing his impatience with a system that limits his power. To the extent that the separation of powers is failing, we risk descending into dictatorship.

Principle Of Liberty #17

Madison wrote, "It will not be denied that power is of an encroaching nature and that it ought to be effectively restrained from passing the limits assigned to it." Modern progressives believe that action is more important than restraint. The unintended consequence is that unrestrained government leads to oppression.

Principle Of Liberty #18

A constitution must be written down in order to be effective. "Put it in writing" is always good advice when you enter into an agreement, and referring back to the written agreement is the best way to stay on track. The Bible tells about a time when "every man did what seemed right in his own eyes". That's human nature. We're in trouble because generations are growing up having not read either Bible or Constitution.

Principle Of Liberty #19

"Only limited and carefully defined powers should be delegated to the government, all others being retained by the people." The modern thought (or lack of thought) is that we can allow the government great authority because the government is us through our vote. The fallacy in this is that government can become so powerful, it can simply say "no" to the people. How many times has the Supreme Court decided that a law passed by the people is unconstitutional? How many times has a Federal law superseded a state law? How often do regulatory agencies simply make up a new rule without asking citizens. You always arrive at a point where the institutions of government separate from the people and become a law unto themselves. Then they are no longer accountable.

Principle Of Liberty #20

We must balance majority versus minority. Efficiency and dispatch require government to operate according to the will of the majority, but Constitutional provisions must protect the rights of the minority. This principle offsets the tyranny of unfettered democracy where the 51 percent force their will on the 49 percent. Just as we should never have enslaved a black minority, we should not vote to tax the "rich" or force Christian medical people to perform abortions. Oppressing minorities is never OK. The majority can allow abortion without forcing everyone to participate. The majority can raise taxes without singling out a minority to pay a greater share.

Principle of Liberty #21

Thomas Jefferson said, "Strong local self-government preserves human freedom. The way to have good and safe government is to not trust it all to one, but to divide it among the many, distributing to every one exactly the functions he is competent to perform best." A liberal friend of mine suggested that human society is evolving and that socialism is the natural next step in that evolution. How foolish. Societal government does not improve by random experimentation, but rather by intelligent design. The founders had just come off a bad experience with tyranny and they wanted nothing to do with another version of tyranny, whether a monarchy or a dictatorship or party rule. They settled on the idea of divided government with checks and balances among its parts. It was a clever way to make government manageable. Liberals and progressives have spent the last 100 years undermining that principle thinking that you can get more done by concentrating power in a presidential dictator. The issue has always been do we need more done or do we need more freedom.

Principle Of Liberty #22

A free people should be governed by law and not by the whims of men. In order for laws to be effective, they must be few and understandable by all. When laws are too many even for the leaders to grasp, leaders begin ruling apart from the law.

Principle Of Liberty #23

A free society cannot survive as a republic without a broad program of general education. When a society and its governing structure is based on principles, the common man must be educated to understand and therefore perpetuate those principles. Americans are to be self-rulers rather than serfs. Whereas slaves can simply we told what to do, we have to be educated to understand what we ought to do.

Principle Of Liberty #24

A free people will not survive unless they stay strong. One of the explicit responsibilities of the federal government is to maintain national defense. There have been competing nations in the world which were not our friends, so we have to protect our country from external tyranny. This principle stands in opposition to the popular notion that America needs to become part of the global community. Community sounds very nice but is extremely naive. America is a sovereign nation with its own character and interests separate from other nations. Other nations have interests in opposition to our own, so we must protect our people from them.

Principle Of Liberty #25

Peace, commerce, and honest friendship with all nations; entangling alliances with none. Some of the trouble the United States experiences involves the expansion of presidential power and the tendency of presidents to assert their personal agenda into foreign affairs. We should not and cannot police the world. Our proper role should be an example of right to other nations through these principles of peace, commerce, and friendship. But in case someone doesn't want to be a friend, see principle 24.

Principle Of Liberty #26

The core unit which determines the strength of any society is the family, therefore the government should foster and protect its integrity. Whereas modern progressives claim to want equality over all other principles, effective government needs to promote useful outcomes. In spite of all the social engineering experiments conducted by educators around the world, there is simply no substitute for the positive influence a mother and father can have on children. The strength of individual families therefore represents a common good for all citizens.

Principle Of Liberty #27

The burden of debt is as destructive to freedom as subjugation by conquest. This is one we know is true, but the love of money makes us ignore it. The federal government is trillions of dollars in debt, and debt advocates say it's not a problem. All we have to do is grow the economy bigger in comparison to what we need to repay. Nevertheless, debt is a chain around our necks. For example, we could promote American manufacturing if we discouraged foreign imports. But to the extent foreign governments are our creditors, we dare not harm them by discouraging their sale of products in our country. In such ways, debt to others creates obligations that limit our freedom and restrict our prosperity.

Principle Of Liberty #28

The United States has a manifest destiny to be an example and a blessing to the entire human race. Do you remember "manifest destiny" from history class? In my day, it referred to the geographical expansion of the United States to the west. Manifest destiny means something more in this case. It means that America is God's representative among nations with a destiny to show the nations the blessings of God brought about by honoring Him in our governing system. That's a bold claim, but one our nation embraced humbly through most of our history. We're not meant to conquer the nations. We're meant to inspire them.

America's Future

America's future seems uncertain, and most Christians are conflicted about it. Although we would love to reverse the decline of America, our understanding of prophesy suggests a world-wide decline leading to an apocalyptic end of days. However, our obligation to both the nations and our neighbors remains. We are servants of the Lord who wants all men to be saved. Our obligation is to preserve and promote the kingdom of God in the culture around us. We are to keep trying.

Irreconcilable

Some political analysts are saying that the crisis of government exists because we have lost the art of "reaching across the aisle" to find points of agreement with the other side. We all have to "move to the center". However, I would question where is the center, and is the center a reasonable goal? Suppose you were observing two football teams each struggling to score. Would it be reasonable to tell them, "Don't try to win, but just get to the 50 yard line and turn the ball over to the other team?" Great. Nobody tries to win, so nobody gets their feelings hurt. All that is lost is success. Is that what moving to the center entails? The conflict in America is between those who love and serve God and those who reject God and want to remove Him from public life. What is the center? Is it lukewarm faith? Is it secularism with religious exceptions? When two worldviews are so diametrically opposed, there is no viable center.

A Social Media Example

I have a social media friend, actually an old business associate/competitor, who reposts anti-Christian and anti-conservative bloggers. I'll call him "Joel" for the sake of confidentiality. Joel might be seen as an old hippy who considers himself a free thinking and technologically savvy modern man. He's an atheist with socialist tendencies blended with a bit of libertarianism. I've always liked Joel.

Joel reposted a blog critical of Republican House Representatives who voted to defund some government social programs. I don't remember the details, but I did record this exact interchange between Joel and me.

Bill: This article seems to underscore what conservatives, libertarians, and constitutionalists have been saying for years; that big government spending and the associated borrowing is unsustainable.

Joel: I thought I remember conservatives (neo-cons) taking us into wars we couldn't afford? I'm not sure I agree with the politicization of the point by saying its 'big govt'. In many ways the govt is too big, in other ways it's too small. In reality it just doesn't serve the people anymore. When govt is too big, they deregulate corporations to cause more harm to society, and they make govt bigger, they make more regs to favor big corps, and make an uphill battle for small business. I think the point of the story is that it looks like it will all be crashing down shortly. I've some articles that say by 2017, but it seems like it will be quicker. But who knows, I've been reading that Bernie Sanders / Elizabeth Warren are getting a lot of support for a pres/vp ticket, which I've been posting since I first saw EW on Bill Maher, so maybe there will be a mass awakening or something.

Joel: Oh, btw, a few months back, I posted an anti-religious article, and you asked me to stop making those sort of posts. I neglected to follow up on that debate. I don't plan on curbing my anti-religion posts, but what got my attention was that you thought it was ok to ask me to stop posting anti-religion stuff. I thought to myself, 'I've got at least 20 or 30 friends hidden from my wall because I don't want to hear their religious crap. It never once occured to me to tell them to stop and control their posts. BUT, you felt it was fine to ask me to stop. To me, that illustrates a key point about the religion insanity, religious people DON'T look at it as their opinion, they look at it as a fact that they are right, and that other people are not being politically correct or culturally sensitive or whatever, when they

> *say anti-christian things. BUT, Christians don't see the need to respect others 1st amendment rights in the same way.*
>
> *Bill: Strange conclusion. I never prohibited you from doing anything. I asked you to consider whether it made sense to forward posts from sites that advocate a distorted view of religion. I prefer your opinions instead of re-posts from unreliable sources. But, I never meant to inhibit your freedom and have no intention of hiding your posts. I find your posts stimulating.*

I got at least one "like" for my response, but the real point is it shows how intertwined and polarizing these issues are. A post about finance turns to politics turns to religion turns to censorship. The center or middle ground is a fiction we use to express our heartfelt desire that we could all just get along. It is the same fiction that weakens our resolve as we combat terrorism or try to fix the economy or seek to restore constitutional government. Radical problems require single-minded solutions. The center is where mediocrity dwells.

It's My Way Or The Highway

Not really, but it's an attention grabbing headline. I began this section with the term "irreconcilable", but now I want to make nice. There is hope for reconciliation, but it involves defeating error in the contest of ideas.

There are people like Joel who seem stuck in wrong thinking. I listened to a talk by Evan Sayet recently, and he said something very perceptive about modern atheistic liberalism. He said that indiscrimination is a moral imperative for liberals because the opposite is discrimination, and discrimination is wrong. In other words, a liberal is opposed to making judgments, even correct judgments, because it would imply that one point of view or one way of behaving is morally superior to another. They don't believe in absolute truth or moral superiority or a better work ethic. The liberal mindset requires that all choices be equally OK. The inevitable result of this thinking is that liberals constantly take the side opposite of Biblical Christianity because Biblical thinking represents an absolute. For example, God instituted the traditional family and research shows that stable families produce the best results in life. That seems unfair to the liberal, so he must champion homosexual marriage, because every kind of family must be equally right.

However, Sayet also observed that life gets in the way of the liberal mindset. For example, if you are a professional athlete, you quickly learn that not any kind of training produces excellent athletic performance. Not just any kind of diet provides the athlete with health and vitality. Not just any kind of attitude allows the athlete to compete exceptionally. Sooner or later, life interferes with the false notion that all behaviors or all thoughts produce equally sound results. It's also important to remember that most atheists are not ideological, but merely naïve. They see it as open-minded or gracious to avoid discrimination or judgment...live and let live. For them also, life will catch up with them and they will see that natural law (the law of God's creation) requires certain favored beliefs and behaviors. So even though the opposite sides, belief in God and rejection of God, are irreconcilable; people will be drawn to reasonable conclusions. Right will win!

An American Mission

We have an obligation as Biblical believers to minister to the people of American and the world's people. President John F. Kennedy once said,

> *"We in this country, in this generation, are, by destiny rather than choice, the watchmen on the walls of world freedom. We ask, therefore, that we may be worthy of our power and responsibility, that we may exercise our strength with wisdom and restraint, and that we may achieve in our time and for all time the ancient vision of peace on earth, goodwill toward men. That must always be our goal-and the righteousness of our cause must always underlie our strength. For as was written long ago, 'Except the Lord keep the city, the watchman waketh but in vain.'"*

As we conclude this brief chapter outlining mankind's struggle against tyranny and the wonderful promise of an America under God, let's agree that what the Lord wants for mankind while man is on the Earth is a moral government that respects and protects the inalienable rights God has given us.

CHAPTER 8

The Christian Gospel

What Is The Gospel?

When Christians refer to the "Gospel" they are referring to the good news that Jesus Christ died to pay the penalty for our sin so that we might become the children of God through faith in Christ alone. He suffered as a sacrifice for sin, overcame death, and now offers a share in His triumph to all who will accept it. The gospel is good news because it is a gift of God, not something that must be earned by ritual or by self-improvement.

The Gospel is not about changing your behavior, becoming a better person or learning to become more moral. It is not even taking the life of Jesus as a model way to live. It is not living highly communal lives with others and sharing generously in communities who practice the way of Jesus in local culture. These may all be good things, but they are not to be confused with the Gospel. All of our works and strivings have nothing to do with what Christ has done for us, but all are about what we propose to do for him. The true Gospel is news about what Christ has already done for us (in his life, death and resurrection) rather than instruction and advice about what you are to do for God.

Do you ever think about Jesus coming as a kind of afterthought of God? Did God only send his son after every other effort failed? Not really. All of the Old Testament pointed to Christ with the first hint in Genesis 3:15. After cursing the serpent God says, "I will put enmity between you and the woman, and between your seed and her seed; he shall bruise your head, and you will bruise his heel." From this passage and many statements by the prophets, a picture is built of a savior born of a virgin who will destroy the enemy of God and his people. God demonstrated through the ancient Hebrews that man was unable to live up to the standard of holy rules, knowing all along that grace was the ultimate answer.

Remember the triangle illustration from the chapter on worldviews? The Gospel brings us full circle to the point of this book. Belief in Jesus Christ has natural consequences regarding the believer's understanding of nature and government...the Biblical worldview. And the natural consequence of a Biblical worldview determines how each of us lives our lives.

Our Challenge

The following is an excerpt from a sermon by Henry Sloan Coffin delivered at the Madison Avenue Presbyterian Church in New York City circa 1915.

> *"An unuttered faith stands in danger of suffocation. Among ourselves thousands of Christians will have little or nothing to do with causes that are distinctly labeled with the Christian name. They are interested in social settlements or philanthropic societies, from which for obvious reasons explicit religious teaching is barred; but they take no part in the work of the Christian church. They can be enlisted for a sewing class or a fresh air outing; but they have no zest for work that involves direct speech on religious subjects. There is a widespread passion for anonymous Christianity. But an unnamed God becomes a forgotten God. Work undertaken originally from religious motives loses its power when one ceases to connect it openly with God. The spiritual tone and force gradually evaporate. An apologetic faith that hides its head soon ceases to possess a believing head worth hiding.*
>
> *This sobering time calls for an end of our hampering shyness in taking God's name and advancing intelligent faith. When one thinks of the state of the world, one is reminded of Hosea's solemn utterance, "My people are destroyed for lack of Knowledge." We must face the fact of abysmal ignorance of the Christian God throughout the earth. Much nominal Christianity has only the faintest connection with the religion of the New Testament. There is a crass superstition; there is a superficial veneer of Christian words over pagan ideals and pagan principles;*

> there is a cynical unbelief among many of us that the kind of deity we read of in the Gospels and talk of in the church is the actual God who is Lord of heaven and earth. Yet there is an urgent summons for believers in God's name to teach Jesus constantly to the ignorant millions in our own and other lands. What possible assurance have we that Americans would not act as ungodly as any other people overseas? Are we willing to pay the cost in personal service, in sacrificial giving, in thoughtful and toilsome re-adaptation of our churches to meet current conditions, that our vast population shall really understand and trust in the name of God? Or shall we wait and pay the cost a thousand fold in some pagan catastrophe like that now turning Europe into a shambles."

What Pastor Coffin was describing is a situation in his day when people were trading their Christian walk for mere good deeds and charitable works. He was calling for a faith that bears fruit that honors the Lord. Both Coffin's day and our own time call for a bold assertion of truth to a world that is sorely in need of it.

You may have learned Jesus quoted as saying "Don't put your light under a bushel, but put it on a candlestick so that it gives light onto all". The science of archaeology sheds light on Jesus' words. Now you might be thinking "what does the Bible have to do with science?" The truth is that scientists investigate a lot of things. Archaeologists who want to learn about the Roman and early Christian era will use the Bible as a guidebook to learn about people and customs of that time.

So let's talk about hiding your light under a bushel. I grew up in an apple-producing region in New York State where every year we would go to the orchard to buy apples in a bushel basket made of wire and thin wood. When I first read the story about a bushel basket in the Bible I always thought "why would anyone put a candle under a bushel basket?" Sounded like a good way to start a fire.

But archaeologists found an artifact of the period that may clarify what Jesus was talking about. The Greek word used in the Bible was "modios", a word that meant a "a measure of dry goods" which was translated as "bushel", an old English measure that we continue to use for such dry goods as apples. The modios may have been something like this. It was designed as a scoop that could be used to scoop grain, but it had a flattened base and top that allowed it to stand up and serve a second purpose. A typical oil lamp of the period could be partnered with the modios. When the lamp wasn't in use, it could be stored in the base of the modios, but when it was lit, it was placed on top of the modios to allow light to radiate all around it. It would be foolish to light the lamp and then hide it in the hollow of the modios where its light would be mostly obstructed.

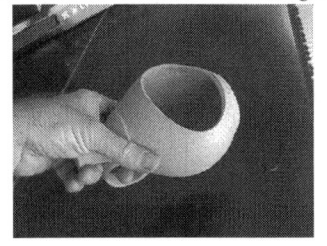

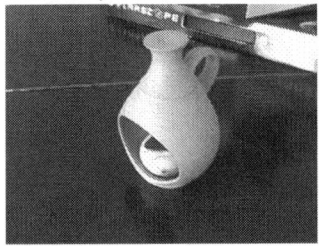

The lesson Jesus was giving wasn't so much religious as it was practical. If you have a skill or an idea or something that could benefit others, don't keep it to yourself. It's your responsibility to share what you have so everyone can benefit. The modios, the Biblical bushel, provided a clear illustration for the people of that time of this lesson. Thanks to the efforts of archaeological scientists we now have a clearer idea of the lesson Jesus was presenting.

Those of us who know Christ have something precious to share. The Gospel isn't about us changing ourselves by our own efforts to make ourselves better. Nevertheless, the effect of the Gospel on us is to change how we live. Consider the lesson of the modios and Pastor Coffin's sermon, and we have a clear indication of our responsibility.

How Should We Then Live?

Many years ago, Dr. Francis Schaeffer wrote a book which subsequently became a documentary series titled "How Should We Then Live". The series documented the rise of western civilization under the influence of Biblical Christianity and the subsequent decline of civilization as Christian influence was removed. Dr. Schaeffer also prophetically predicted the rise of a manipulative elite to replace the Christian consensus, a future we are now seeing unfold. He concluded that the only hope to restore the freedoms afforded by the Christian worldview was for people to restore their individual commitment to the truths of God; that God is real, that He has spoken clearly to us, and that we have an obligation to honor Him and spread the Gospel to the world. What Dr. Schaeffer didn't explain is exactly what that looks like beyond an intellectual concept. Exactly how do we live both individually and collectively as the Church? How do we educate new believers? How do we support fellow believers spiritually and materially? How do we reach out beyond the church, influence the culture, and draw people to the knowledge of God?

First, let me follow a brief aside and talk about who the church is. During the first century of the New Testament, the church simply was a collective term for a body of believers. As separate bodies grew up geographically, the term came to be used for collections of believers in different communities as in the church of Corinth or the church of Galatia. As time went on, churches became institutional bodies which now have evolved into denominations and local fellowships. Lately there has been a movement to get away from the notion of church institutions and nurture small fellowships for more intimate relationship and deeper accountability. I don't think any of these variations are important in terms of being the "right" structure. What is important is that we have a Biblical mandate to fellowship collectively, and there are many things that we can do collectively more effectively than we can accomplish alone. Let's agree then that when I say "church", I mean any body of believers who have joined together in submission to Christ in any form they find meaningful. We are the church.

What is the role of the Church then? It is clearly beyond the individual and personal, although the collective church would certainly be a nurturing environment for every individual. The church's role has two main dimensions; one directed inward toward the support of fellow believers and the second aimed outward to save the unsaved. The church is incomplete without both dimensions fully and consciously in play.

So let's outline what this looks like in terms of how each of us should live within the church and what we should be doing. Basically, everything begins with the individual but the church collective supplements when individual action is inadequate.

- Each individual is called to seek the Lord. God is a rewarder of those who seek Him and the Spirit draws people to Him. However you came to accept Jesus as your Lord, you've embarked on a life long journey of discovery. Very little knowledge is needed to become a Christian and

witness to others, but you should feel excited to learn more by reading the Bible daily and being exhorted by more mature believers.
- You have a personal responsibility to your children. You want your children to be saved and they are designed to copy you. Let them see Christ in you in everyday living. Talk about things of the Lord regularly and casually applying what you know to everyday events.
- You have an obligation to serve the church. While some churches take a legalistic stance on eldership as an office or position, mature Christians are all elders. The obligation of those who are older is to teach, exhort, and minister to younger believers, never as lords over them, but as credible examples demonstrating how we should live.
- You must reach out to the lost. Some people in ministry wonder why participation in church is down and cite all kinds of sociological reasons. Maybe, however, it's because modern Christians rarely share the gospel with non-believers and we aren't growing new members. Be an active worker in you church's outreach programs. Counsel your children toward careers that can impact the culture and draw people to Christ. Understand also that the goal is not really new church members. The goal is to save lives through the saving power of Jesus Christ. They'll probably come to church after that.

The role of the church supplements the activity of individuals. Church isn't a substitute for the life of each individual. What the church does is enable united believers to have impacts greater than individuals can achieve.
- The church provides a mechanism to build up the individual. This is the first dimension of collective church responsibility. We are called to fellowship at least in part because fellowship is the mechanism for building up each individual. How better will children and new converts be exposed to the knowledge of God than by exposure to mature believers speaking into their lives. The church also lets us worship together. The most tangible role played by the church is meeting together for corporate worship and fellowship. Even the smallest congregation with the least amount of resources and programs fulfills the basic need of Christians to worship God together. Worship provides the venue for each individual to experience and share the gifts of the Spirit among the body

of believers. Church fulfills the desire of God for worship and man for relationship. The church should be a place of refuge for believers growing toward maturity. Note that the primary school for spiritual growth is the family, but church is the safety net. At least some new converts don't have a Christian family or a mentor to guide them. In such cases, the church becomes their spiritual family both guiding and holding them accountable in their new walk. However, even for mature believers, the church offers a place to connect with the deeper knowledge that only comes from exposure to great teachers. To summarize, the church is a safety net to disciple new believers and an environment for advanced studies.

- The church provides a material safety net for its members. Just as in the spiritual, every individual is responsible for their own material welfare, but everyone needs help sometime. The New Testament explicitly names widows and orphans as dependents who should be cared for by the church. It also implies the kind of mutual support system exemplified by Acts where everyone sold what they had and shared among the collective. We don't need to take this as a call for communal living, but simply as an example of Christian cooperation. For the last few decades, the church has delegated this role of the church to secular government's social welfare systems. We know it's wrong because we have seen how secular programs try to perform Godly charity without allowing God to participate. The church cares for the helpless. The New Testament differentiates between widows who need assistance and those who don't. It's not important to go into that here, but there is a clear instruction for the church to help those in real need. Elderly unmarried widows should be on every church's radar with a clear effort to provide companionship, financial assistance, and volunteer effort to help with any home maintenance a single woman can't do herself. This has to be more than a nice idea or good intent. It has to be a regular effort. The church also supports individuals in emergencies. Employment is primarily an individual responsibility, but there needs to be a safety net when there's a disruption in the economy or a personal disability. We're not against the programs of secular government, but those are not the preferred solutions. Far better that brother help brother, and the church can help organize that process. Churches should keep an inventory of business owners who can offer employment to the church's unemployed. If a church has no members who own prosperous businesses (increasingly common), the church should consider establishing a church-wide enterprise. This doesn't need to be run by the church, but can be assigned to members who have an entrepreneurial bent. Does your church have a lot of members with building and maintenance skills? Why not offer to the community a property management and maintenance service that employs your pool of members in times of need? Is this the proper role of church? Consider the story of the good Samaritan and who Jesus said was the man's brother. His brother was the one who helped the man in need.

- The church supports outreach. Changing the world one person at a time is the second area of collective responsibility. The emphasis of the book of Acts is about evangelists like Paul preaching the Gospel to the unbelieving community and building the early church. By contrast, the modern mature church spends the bulk of its resources on building up the internal community with only minimal contact with the unbelieving community outside. This worked while America was a primarily Christian nation, but it won't work any more. If salvation is what we say it is, then we must have a burden for all people to be saved. Not everyone has the manner and methods of an evangelist, but the church includes evangelists who can teach the methods of evangelism to the rest. Consider the Way Of The Master series featuring Ray Comfort and Kirk Cameron who team up to demonstrate how to engage non-believers in discussing their need for a savior. Programs like this can be used to teach Christians how to witness, but those new skills need to be exercised. The church must develop and conduct group events in the community that allow members to engage with the public in presenting the Gospel. Sharing Christ is a skill and a habit that becomes easier with repetition and the church collectively provides a secure way to do this.

- The church manages and directs volunteers. Because the church has been largely absent from evangelism, individuals have struck out on their own to create quasi-church ministry outreaches into the community. Unfortunately, because these ministries were formed separate from "the church", they are sometimes not embraced by members of the church. But there's another reason Christians don't participate in outreach ministries and I'll use my CreationXpo ministry as an example. A leader of a missionary organization came in one day to examine our creation worldview exhibition and concluded, "We don't really need this because we already know about creation." In other words, "There isn't anything in this for me." Unfortunately, most Christians don't look at outreach in terms of the outreach. They accepted Christ in order to save themselves and they attend church because they "enjoy the fellowship" or "love the music" or "want to be fed". Intellectually and doctrinally we know that the Christian walk isn't all about me, but the church has been so inward-directed for so long that self absorption has become our habit. If we can change that mindset, the good news is that working at a ministry outreach is a great way for the non-evangelist to reach out to non-Christians. The church's role in this is to encourage participation as one of the ways Christians can fulfill the Great Commission.

- The church serves its community by getting involved outside of the church. For example, engagement in politics isn't normally considered spiritual, but infusing the political realm with Godly men and women is certainly an aspect of representing the church in the conflict over ideas. Or consider a company like Chick-Fil-A whose primary purpose is to sell chicken and make money, but also makes it clear they are followers of Jesus and in that way testifies to the power of the Lord in their business success. We are called to not be of the world, but certainly to be in it; and the world is better off for our presence to the extent that we reflect our Lord even through ordinary things. Every church should encourage its members, particularly its young people, to infiltrate the culture in every way possible so that ignorant people might become aware of God's kingdom around them.

What I've presented here is not just a set of principles or some nice ideas. We must put this into action as the church. Church "programs" have been criticized in recent years for being impersonal or manipulative, but we do need structure and direction in the church. Every church should have these goals clearly stated, and every pastor should constantly refer to all these components of "how we should then live". It should not be an option for members of the church to not be involved in at least one activity that extends beyond their individual life.

The complete Gospel is more than just the individual being saved. The Gospel is a replicating process where individuals receive the free gift of salvation through our Lord Jesus Christ and are empowered and inspired to share that free gift with others.

Conclusion

Many great teachers have called upon the church to be unified, but the greatest of all was our Lord. Jesus' words are recorded in Mark 9:38, "John said to him, Master, we saw one driving out evil spirits in your name: and we said that he should not, because he is not one of us. But Jesus said, Say not so: for there is no man who will do a great work in my name, and be able at the same time to say evil of me. He who is not against us is for us." The Lord was expressing inclusiveness, being slow to divide over doctrinal details. Jesus added another dimension in John 13:34, "A new command I give you that you love one another as I have loved you. By this all men shall know that you are my disciples, that you love one another." The Lord said these things to ensure that believers in Him would walk in unity being gracious to one another.

Much of this book has been about practical matters like science and government. Why should we care about creation science? It's certainly not because of mere theories about origins. The issue is truth, and that atheistic science has stolen the Bible from the Church. Where God's Word was the rock foundation of Christianity, our source of confidence; now we can't agree on what it really says. Well-meaning Christian leaders began to reinterpret Genesis to accommodate what they thought science had proven. Then the next generation of Biblical scholars said, "If Genesis can't be taken at face value or if Moses simply borrowed the creation story from Babylon, perhaps other Bible stories are mythology." That generation questioned the truth of God's Word. Subsequent generations simply dismissed the Bible as unimportant. After all, we're saved by grace aren't we? Why do the Scriptures matter?

The issue is truth and the consequences of ideas. What is it that believers are to believe? I have two friends who consider themselves to be prophetically gifted, and there is no doubt that they love the Lord and seek after Him daily. Nevertheless, these two who are tuned to the Holy Spirit have completely different ideas about creation and reality. For some, such disagreements cause them to lose confidence in the effectiveness of the Spirit in revealing truth, but I see it differently. The Spirit speaks with revelatory power, but the world system has spoken confusion even to the saints. It's time to reject confusion, seek clarity, and restore truth.

In many ways, the deeper issue is about community. If Christians are to survive and thrive in the years ahead, we must join together as a community of believers for mutual support and to minister corporately to a lost world. To accomplish this, we start with the truth. We become champions of the truth, We resist our human, fallen call to fragmentation and division. We repent and turn to the God of creation. The full nature of this community, what it looks like and how it operates, is the subject of another day. Nevertheless, community is the goal.

For Bible Believers

This book has covered a broad spectrum of ideas, in fact everything that would constitute a consistent worldview. However, it would be naïve to expect every Bible-believing reader to simply drop their long cherished beliefs and accept what I have laid out. What I am suggesting is more subtle, but every bit as decisive. What I am suggesting is that Bible believers should adopt an "orthodox" standard of beliefs while each individual remains free to consider and pursue their personal doubts and directions. I read an ebook recently about Jewish theology (sorry, I can't cite the author or title). The Jewish teacher asserted a fundamental distinction between Judaism and Christianity in that Jews have many rabbinical schools, but they don't easily divide over doctrine. Jewish people emphasize their common identity rather than their intellectual disagreements.

What I have laid out in these pages ties together our shared faith with the rational consequences of that faith in the sciences and social institutions. Every element is rationally defensible, yet every point is arguable. You may, for example, personally believe that the Earth is older than a few thousand years, but I suspect you can't easily refute the Biblical chronology I presented that establishes human history as just a few thousand years old. Over the last century and a half, Christians have allowed humanist ideas to infiltrate our worldview. It happened because the church was unprepared to defend Biblical thinking in the natural and social sciences. However, the church compromised its belief system prematurely. We now have modern creationist concepts to re-assert the Biblical framework.

I am not suggesting that we turn back the clock and return to the good old days. The truth is that throughout the so-called church age, true Biblical Christianity has never been ascendant. It's always been overshadowed by the distortion of human religion. Biblical thinking is therefore a new revolution...a bold attempt to set man's thinking aside and defer to God's truth. I'm suggesting we hold to what I have presented throughout this book as a standard for investigation. Whatever truth this book contains is not to be credited to the human author, but to the ultimate authority. Let's adopt it unless we can prove it wrong. This approach allows you to hold on to your individual doubts while also honoring a collective standard. Let's emphasize the beliefs which unite us. God is the Creator, and the Bible outlines the creative process and a relatively short term of human history. Let's be gracious in accepting each other's challenging ideas while maintaining a unified face to the world as children of God who love one another. It is only through unity that we can transform the world's thinking and save its lost souls. It's only through unity that we can become the unblemished bride that Christ desires. It's only through unity that each of us individually can be encouraged and edified.

For Non Believers And Skeptics

This book's message for skeptics is that Bible believers have a well-reasoned basis for what they believe. Never dare think that your position is founded on reason or science. That delusion lets you off too easy. Understanding what is true requires much more than a blind faith in all things scientific sounding. I encourage you to consider the world as you would like it to be, and then consider if that vision might not be the Spirit of God drawing you to embrace your true identity. It's only natural. You are, after all, created in His image.

Some Choices Are Simple

"See, I have set before you today life and prosperity, and death and adversity; in that I command you today to love the Lord your God, to walk in His ways and to keep His commandments and His statutes and His judgments, that you may live and multiply, and that the Lord your God may bless you in the land where you are entering to possess it. But if your heart turns away and you will not obey, but are drawn away and worship other gods and serve them, I declare to you today that you shall surely perish. You will not prolong your days... I call heaven and earth to witness against you today, that I have set before you life and death, the blessing and the curse. So choose life in order that you may live, you and your descendants, by loving the Lord your God, by obeying His voice, and by holding fast to Him; for this is your life and the length of your days..." Deuteronomy 30:15-20

Bibliography

Dr. Francis Schaefer	How Should We Then Live: Crossway 1976
Dr. Russell Humphreys	Starlight And Time: Master Books 1996
Guillermo Gonzalez and Jay Richards.	The Privileged Planet: Regnery Publishing 2004
D. James Kennedy	The Real Meaning Of The Zodiac: Coral Ridge 1989
H&M Stix and R. T. Abbott	The Shell: Five Hundred Million Years Of Inspired Design: BDD Promotional Book 1991
Charles Lyell	Principles Of Geology: 1830
Charles Darwin	Origin Of Species By Natural Selection 1859
Dr. Samuel Turner	Companion To The Book Of Genesis 1841
Philip Mauro	Wonders Of Bible Chronology 1934
Dr. Walt Brown	In The Beginning: Center For Scientific Creation 2008
Vance Nelson	Dire Dragons: Self Published 2011
Cleon Skousen	The 5,000 Year Leap: National Center For Constitutional Studies 1991

Index

believer, 2, 8, 9, 10, 11, 15, 42, 132, 146
Big Bang, 15, 17, 23, 25, 32, 42, 46, 47, 48, 51, 52, 53, 55
Cosmology
  cosmology, 25, 41, 46, 51, 52, 53
Creator, 1, 3, 4, 7, 8, 9, 11, 12, 25, 27, 28, 31, 33, 50, 78, 80, 81, 82, 83, 85, 92, 115, 131, 133, 157
dinosaurs, 15, 77, 103, 117, 118, 119, 120, 121, 122, 123, 124, 125, 126
dragons, 117, 120, 121, 123, 124, 125, 126
geology, 43, 95, 96, 97, 98, 99, 104, 106, 107, 114, 116
Gospel
  gospel, 22, 56, 57, 58, 145, 146, 148, 149, 152, 154
government, 1, 5, 6, 7, 8, 9, 10, 11, 12, 13, 14, 15, 21, 128, 129, 130, 131, 132, 133, 134, 135, 136, 137, 138, 139, 140, 141, 142, 143, 146, 151, 155

humanist, 5, 9, 10, 11, 12, 13, 15, 17, 18, 22, 23, 24, 27, 28, 30, 38, 43, 49, 52, 73, 76, 83, 129, 157
Hydroplate Theory, 110, 111, 112
life, 7, 1, 2, 3, 5, 10, 11, 14, 19, 25, 30, 36, 50, 56, 71, 72, 73, 74, 76, 77, 78, 79, 80, 81, 82, 83, 84, 95, 98, 99, 102, 103, 105, 106, 132, 140, 142, 143, 145, 149, 150, 154, 158
truth, 2, 6, 10, 12, 13, 14, 15, 18, 21, 22, 29, 31, 32, 33, 43, 44, 69, 96, 98, 100, 133, 142, 147, 155, 156, 157
universe, 5, 13, 16, 17, 22, 23, 24, 25, 26, 28, 32, 41, 42, 43, 44, 45, 46, 47, 48, 49, 50, 51, 52, 53, 54, 55, 56, 69, 71, 80, 95
worldview, 1, 2, 3, 5, 7, 8, 9, 10, 11, 13, 14, 15, 17, 19, 20, 21, 22, 23, 26, 28, 31, 32, 38, 73, 129, 146, 148, 153, 156, 157

ABOUT THE AUTHOR

Bill Mundhausen is the Chairman of the corporation and Director of day-to-day operations of Orion Center. Bill was born in Rhinebeck, New York in 1949 and grew up in nearby Barrytown...a community on the Hudson River about 90 miles north of New York City. He attended college at the University of Rochester and San Francisco State College graduating with a Bachelor of Arts in English Literature in 1971.The Orion Center developed the CreationXpo Biblical Worldview Center with an emphasis on the foundational place of the Bible in science, society, and individual life.

Made in the USA
Charleston, SC
30 August 2015